Philosophy of Song and Singing

In *Philosophy of Song and Singing: An Introduction*, Jeanette Bicknell explores key aesthetic, ethical, and other philosophical questions that have not yet been thoroughly researched by philosophers, musicologists, or scientists. Issues addressed include:

- The relationship between the meaning of a song's words and its music;
- The performer's role and the ensuing complications for gender social ontology and personal identity;
- The performer's ethical obligations to audiences, composers, lyricists, and those for whom the material holds particular significance;
- The metaphysical status of isolated solo performances compared with the continuous singing of opera or the interrupted singing of stage and screen musicals.

Each chapter focuses on one major musical example and includes several shorter discussions of other selections. All have been chosen for their illustrative power and their accessibility for any interested reader and are readily available.

Jeanette Bicknell is an independent scholar based in Toronto, Canada. She is the author of *Why Music Moves Us* (2009) and is the co-editor (with John Andrew Fisher) of *Song, Songs, and Singing* (2013).

Philosophy of Song and Singing
An Introduction

Jeanette Bicknell

Routledge
Taylor & Francis Group

LONDON AND NEW YORK

First published 2015
by Routledge
711 Third Avenue, New York, NY 10017

and by Routledge
2 Park Square, Milton Park, Abingdon, Oxon OX14 4RN

*Routledge is an imprint of the Taylor & Francis Group, an informa
business*

© 2015 Taylor & Francis

Library of Congress Cataloging in Publication Data
Bicknell, Jeanette.
A philosophy of song and singing : an introduction / Jeanette Bicknell.
pages cm
Includes bibliographical references and index.
1. Singing--Philosophy. 2. Songs--Philosophy and aesthetics. I. Title.
ML3872.B53 2015
783'.01--dc23
2014048862

ISBN: 978-1-138-79066-7 (hbk)
ISBN: 978-1-138-79067-4 (pbk)
ISBN: 978-1-315-76405-4 (ebk)

Typeset in Sabon
by Taylor & Francis

The only thing better than singing is more singing.

Ella Fitzgerald

Contents

Preface

I grew up in a musical household. I studied the violin from childhood and took up the trombone in high school. I was fortunate to be exposed to a wide variety of music on the radio and through my parents' record collection. I played in a youth orchestra, in bands at school, and in the local community band. My sister and brother also played musical instruments. Yet despite all this music-making and listening, I didn't really understand singing or even think much about singing until I took singing lessons as an adult. And I took singing lessons for the most non-musical of reasons. A recent PhD graduate in philosophy and in the early stages of an academic career, I knew that I would most likely have to teach large classes at some point. (No one seems to escape this.) I heard somewhere (and I don't know if this is true) that the historian Simon Schama would, on the first day of his British History class, sing "Rule Britannia" (all verses) to the crowd of assembled students. Not something I would attempt, but I thought maybe Schama was on to something. Maybe singing lessons would help me use my voice more effectively in front of large classes. And so I signed up for a group singing class at the Royal Conservatory of Music.

Although the class was group instruction, we were each encouraged to choose songs to work on with the teacher, to sing for each other in class, and eventually to perform solo at the end-of-term recital. One of the first songs I picked was the Rogers and Hart standard, "It Never Entered My Mind." I knew the song through Sarah Vaughn's recording and it had long been a favorite.[1] I bought the sheet music and was eager to see on paper a song that I thought I knew fairly well. So I was pretty confused when I began to study the score and found something markedly different from what I expected. Where the score had notes of equal value, Vaughn made some slightly longer than others, emphasizing some words at the expense of others. Where the score had a single pitch (as on the word "easy" in the line "uneasy in my easy chair"), Vaughn adds melisma (that is, she varies the pitch within a single syllable). Where the score has one note follow another directly, Vaughn pauses between them, making the listener eager to hear the continuation. After a little research I learned that the song – like so many jazz standards – had its origin in a Broadway musical. I gained a new appreciation for how Vaughn takes the somewhat silly lyrics ("I don't care if my hairdo is in place," etc.) and makes them tinged with pathos. While I had always loved her performance, I now began to appreciate what a significant *musical* achievement it was.

My late interest in singing seems all the more surprising when I think that, by the time I started to think seriously about it, I had already written a dissertation on the topic of understanding music and I would soon begin a research project on strong emotional experiences of music (which eventually became my first book, *Why Music Moves Us*). But maybe this isn't so surprising after all. While the last 30 years or so have seen a surge of interest in the philosophy of music, with some recent and important exceptions, there is still comparatively little philosophical literature on singing. This lack is especially evident within the tradition of analytic aesthetics, my philosophical home. Philosophers have tended to assume that instrumental music provides the greatest philosophical challenges and they have underestimated the philosophical importance and complexity of songs and singing. When philosophers have written about singing they have tended to confine their inquiries to specific artistic genres. So there has been philosophical examination of singing in opera, singing in the rock tradition, and the vocal aspect of rap music, but very little consideration of what might be common to singing across different musical and cultural traditions.

The practice of singing is both widespread and taken for granted, and I have come to think that it is probably both the most popular and the least understood musical activity. While I have not done a survey, I would predict that more amateur musicians sing than play any instrument, and that singers are the most famous and financially successful of musicians. Singing is at once an artistic pursuit, a leisure pastime, and a staple of the mass entertainment industry. It is also a cultural practice with a role in all societies we know of, and the practice of singing to infants likely played a significant part in human evolutionary history. Yet, unlike any other performing art, mass entertainment, or cultural practice, singing involves text, melody, and an embodied subject or subjects. Singing thus raises distinctive philosophical, aesthetic, and ethical concerns. These have not been explored thoroughly by philosophers or by scientists.

The conventional understanding of singing sees it as a form of communication; but with reflection the communication paradigm becomes unsatisfactory. In a song, what is communicated, and to whom? Why sing to communicate when spoken words are likely to be more readily understood? Rather, singing is a complex social institution. Understood in this way, we can create a framework for understanding it, researching into it, and thinking ethically about it that goes against the grain of received and popular understandings.

The Structure of This Book

Following Cartesian principles of beginning with simple matters and going on to greater complexity, the first chapter is about words in songs. The presence of a text sets songs apart from other types of music. We'll see that song texts, especially those of mass and popular art, tend to be redundant and to trade in familiar simplifications. Traditional song texts (including children's songs, lullabies, ballads, and blues songs) bear marks of oral communication. They are often repetitive, redundant, highly malleable, and exist in numerous versions. I consider some philosophical ramifications for the ontological status of songs, for their identity conditions, and for song meaning.

The second chapter adds music to words. What do words and music do for one another, and what is the proper construal of the relationship between the meaning of a song's words and its melodic structure? I consider previous philosophical writing on this topic, including work by Aaron Ridley, Jerrold Levinson, and others. Music can reinforce words or undercut them. It can bring our attention to some words at the expense of others.

There is no music without performers, and Chapter 3 begins the consideration of singers and what they do. Asking what singers do might seem too obvious a move. Yet while singing is a physical activity, it is at the same time a social and cultural activity, and some singing is an art form. Singing is subject to a variety of collective expectations and takes place within specific shared contexts. With these factors in mind, what makes singing different from other types of vocal performance? What are the general criteria for *successful* song performance?

Since what a singer does when he or she sings will depend on the expectations of both the singer and those in attendance, Chapters 4 through 7 consider the relationship between singers and audiences in some depth. In Chapter 4 I develop the concept of the singer's "public persona" and argue that incongruities may be raised if there is a disconnect between what the song communicates and that persona. Public singing performances involve complex issues of gender, social ontology, and personal identity, and, in some cases, they invoke for audiences the value of "authenticity." Chapter 5 begins with some ground clearing before turning to authenticity in music. I propose three different ways to think about authenticity in vocal music, and I also consider what kind of a value "authenticity" is. Is it something inherent in music or performance, the way that the authenticity of a painting by Picasso or Rembrandt might be inherent in it? And how do we decide whether or not a particular musical artist or performance is truly "authentic" or not?

Chapter 6 continues the discussion of authenticity in a different form. Technological innovations in music have inspired some of the concerns about authenticity. Auto-tune is probably the most controversial of these innovations, and I also consider amplification in opera and the use of pre-recorded tracks in live performance. Chapter 7 goes deeper into the relationship between singers and audiences, considering singers' ethical obligations.

Since so much vocal music is found within the context of music drama – whether opera, Broadway musicals or film – Chapter 8 is devoted to song and drama. Although I discuss different forms of music drama, I have the most to say about opera. I find opera particularly interesting because it can be seen as the "extreme" form of musical drama, and so the problems of song and drama come out most sharply here. Also, it is probable that more philosophers have written about opera than have written about other forms of vocal music.

The final two chapters are, in a sense, where all the previous chapters have been leading. They are about meaning: first, how to think about the meaning of songs, and next, what meaning singing has in people's lives. Is the meaning of a song to be found in its text, in its music, in their conjunction, or in the tension between them? The account of musical meaning I develop applies to a particular class of song – those songs that are works for performance and that are sung in performance. For such songs, I argue, meaning is a product of three factors: the song's text, its music, and the performance context. Meaning is co-created by performers and listeners, within specific contexts. The final chapter takes up the question of why people sing. A strange question, to be sure. Yet I hope that you'll appreciate its richness after having progressed with me throughout the previous chapters.

Each chapter has at least one major musical example, plus several shorter discussions of other examples. I have selected examples for their illustrative power and their accessibility. All should be readily available on the internet. I hope you will pause while reading to listen to or watch at least a few of them.

The most glaring omissions that readers are likely to notice is that I say too little about choral music, far too little about non-Western music, and nothing about duet singing. I can only apologize for these shortcomings and encourage others to continue the discussion.

Notes

1 www.youtube.com/watch?v=u37lgz7b3lQ

Acknowledgements

Many people took the time to discuss with me the ideas developed in this book, and I am grateful to all of them. As an "independent scholar" working without institutional support, I have been fortunate to have a network of philosophical and musical friends and associates who patiently answered my (sometimes naïve) questions, commented on drafts, provided encouragement, drew my attention to relevant music and writings, and more than made up for the lack of an institutional home base. So it is a pleasure to thank an anonymous reviewer for Routledge, Kathy Behrendt, Jim Davies, Leslie Fink, Ted Gracyk, Justin London, Randy Metcalfe, and Joel Rudinow.

I owe special debts of gratitude to Jennifer Judkins, who read and commented on the entire manuscript; John Andrew Fisher, my co-editor on the *Journal of Aesthetics and Art Criticism*'s special issue on song and singing, who read and commented on much of the manuscript; and Jerrold Levinson, who encouraged my earliest forays into these topics while I was a post doctoral fellow at the University of Maryland. Each has been an invaluable "conversationalist" and has probably influenced me more than they realize.

I believe that philosophical aesthetics is enriched when philosophers engage with practicing artists and performers. So I am particularly grateful to pianist and educator Charlie Kert, who helped me with many musical questions; Adria McCulloch, who shared with me her experience of the world of opera and art song; and Nancy Zeligman, who was a great source of information about the performance of jazz and popular song. The book gained substantially from their input.

Finally, I would like to acknowledge the patience, support, and input of my husband, Ian Jarvie, and my daughter, Madeleine Eleanor Jarvie. Both were sources of inspiration, with interesting insights about song and singing. This book is dedicated to them.

1   Words

Words set songs apart from other musical forms, and the requirement to communicate words sets singers apart from other musicians. So we will start with words.

There was singing before there were musical instruments, before there was writing, and before there was musical notation. There may even have been singing before there was speech. We do not know what the first "songs" sounded like. Did they originate in threats howled in imitation of an animal's cadence? Or perhaps in a mother's reassuring syllables, crooned and repeated until a lilting melody took shape? Despite how little we know about the origins of singing, it seems plausible that one early function of singing was oral communication. Song texts continue to be shaped by the burdens and limitations of oral communication, and this makes them different from other kinds of texts that do not assume oral communication.

Songs as Oral Communication

The function of oral communication has shaped song texts in many ways. We can most readily see how if we focus on traditional songs (including children's songs, lullabies, spirituals, ballads, work songs and blues songs). The oldest of these songs pre-date the development of mass media publication and recording. They were distributed in pre-literate cultures, by being taught by one singer to another and by one generation of singers to the next. Although the marks of oral communication can be seen most obviously in traditional songs, the traces of oral communication remain evident in songs composed since the advent of mass communication, recording technology, and near-universal literacy.

Perhaps the most obvious legacy of song's function as oral communication is in the use of repetition. A glance at a traditional songbook makes it clear that such song texts are often highly repetitive. Single words are repeated and the same line (or very close variations) are repeated. The same chorus is typically sung after every verse, and the verses and choruses themselves may be highly repetitive. A traditional song's verses and chorus may consist of the same line (or very close variations) repeated a number of times.

A few examples: in the traditional Scottish folk song "My Bonnie Lies over the Ocean" each verse consists of one line (or a close variation) repeated three times:

> My bonnie lies over the ocean
> My bonnie lies over the sea
> My bonnie lives over the ocean
> Oh bring back my bonnie to me

In the four lines of the chorus the phrase "Bring back" is repeated six times:

> Bring back, bring back, bring back my bonnie to me, to me
> Bring back, bring back, oh bring back my bonnie to me

The American spiritual "He's Got the Whole World in His Hands" repeats the words of the title four times in each chorus and again as the last line of each verse. Each verse itself consists of a line repeated three times, followed by "He's got the whole world in His hands."

In the children's song "She'll be Coming Round the Mountain" each verse is four lines long, a single line is repeated for three of the four, and the one contrasting line is simply a shorter variation of the repeated line:

> She'll be coming round the mountain when she comes
> She'll be coming round the mountain when she comes
> She'll be coming round the mountain, she'll be coming round the mountain
> She'll be coming round the mountain when she comes

To make the song even more repetitive every line ends with the words "when she comes."

Repetition is not limited to children's songs or folk songs. Consider Handel's "Hallelujah Chorus" from his oratorio *Messiah*:

> And He shall reign forever and ever,
> King of kings! and Lord of lords!
> And He shall reign forever and ever,
> King of kings! and Lord of lords!
> Hallelujah! Hallelujah! Hallelujah! Hallelujah! Hallelujah!

Next, song texts are redundant. This means that a song's lyrics will convey the same information a number of times in a number of different ways. "My bonnie lies over the ocean" and "My bonnie lies over the sea" convey essentially the same information. In the gospel song "Down by the Riverside," the lines of the chorus ("Ain't gonna study war no more") are reinforced by other lines with similar declarations of personal pacifism: "I'm gonna lay down my sword and shield," "Gonna stick my sword in the golden sand," and "Gonna walk with the Prince of Peace." Similarly, if we already know that He's got "the whole world" in his hands then any further elaboration ("the wind and the rain," "you and me") is redundant.

Traditional songs often exist in numerous versions. The song I learned as "Go Tell Aunt Rhody" is known elsewhere as "Go Tell Aunt Nancy" and "Go Tell Aunt Tempie." Cecil Sharp's *Collection of English Folk Songs* records eight different versions of a song called "The Foggy Dew" (not to be confused with several traditional Irish ballads with the same title). And dozens of versions of the traditional English song "Scarborough Fair" existed by the end of the eighteenth century.[1] Even when there is a widely accepted "standard" version of a traditional song, it may be altered in performance. Verses may be dropped or sung out of order, and lyrics may be changed to accommodate a change of narrator from male to female or vice versa.

How greatly a song's lyrics may be changed in performance is often a cultural, music-cultural, or stylistic matter. Not all genres allow for as much variation as do traditional songs. Not a word of Schumann's *Dichterliebe* or a Mozart duet may be changed at the singer's whim. Generally speaking, the more a song is considered a work of "classical" or "art" music, the more rigid is its text. The great American songwriter and composer Cole Porter was said to become upset if singers embellished or altered his lyrics. (There is a story that he refused to shake Frank Sinatra's hand when the latter added the line "You give me a boot" to Porter's song "I Get a Kick out of You"). Yet Porter was compelled to change a line in the same song when the stage musical for which it was written was made into a film in 1936. "Some get a kick from cocaine" became "Some like the perfume in Spain" to comply with Hollywood's 1930 Production Code.

"I Get a Kick out of You" is only one example of how social factors and changing cultural norms and attitudes influence how song texts are conveyed in performance. Another example is found in the Rolling Stones' classic "Brown Sugar." One of the most elusive and ambiguous texts in rock music, the song is often interpreted as celebrating black women and has also been criticized for what are taken to be insensitive references to slavery. In the original, 1971 recording, Mick Jagger sings the last line of the first verse as "Hear him whip the women just around midnight." Today casual remarks about the brutality of slavery are not heard in the same way and society is less accepting of violence against women. So that is presumably why when the Stones have performed the song more recently (as seen in many live versions on the internet) Jagger omits the reference to whipping and sings instead "You should have heard me just around midnight."

Trivially, traditional songs were cognitively and musically accessible to the people who composed and sang them. This accessibility goes hand-in-hand with a reliance on familiar forms, which is shared by more recent songs as well. The distinction between traditional songs and art songs, composed and performed by musical elites or professionals, emerges only with the development of musical notation. One reason for repetition and the use of familiar forms is that it makes songs easier to remember. Along with this reliance on widely known musical forms, traditional songs take as their subjects topics that would have been of interest to most or all of the community, or their singing performs functions that would have been important to many. The subjects of traditional songs include the vagaries of love, personal salvation, the hardship of life, and important historical or cultural events. Some of the functions performed or assisted by singing traditional songs, whether alone or in groups, include calming or entertaining children, facilitating the rhythms of shared work, marking important occasions, and aiding in the retention of important information.

What of the merit or value (whether literary, philosophical, or aesthetic) of song texts? Many if not most traditional and popular songs do not fare well if judged by literary standards, although there are exceptions. Traditional and popular songs rarely ask either listeners or singers to depart from their intellectual or musical comfort zones. Guitarist, songwriter, and Rolling Stones co-founder Keith Richards put this well when he was asked about the meaning of his song "Wild Horses": "Once you've got the vision in your mind of wild horses, I mean, what's the next phrase you're going to use? It's got to be 'couldn't drag me away.'"[2]

In Britain, when folk song collecting began in earnest in the late nineteenth century, sneers at the "quality" of song texts were combined with admiration for traditional tunes.[3] Indeed, the primary focus of many of these and other folk song collectors in different areas was music, not words. A tendency to denigrate song texts – especially those of traditional or popular songs – often combined with a patronizing attitude to those who sang them, is found frequently in music and cultural criticism. Then, as now, simply quoting the text of a song may be presented as sufficient for anyone to recognize its banality. Discomfort with the "coarseness" or vulgarity of traditional songs also hampered their collection. Editors of folk song collections expurgated without qualms. "The coarseness of the original words obliged me to re-write the song," one editor tells us. The charge of vulgarity is, of course, still made of popular song texts today.

A condescending attitude to the music and songs that one takes to be alien is, I feel, more complex than may be generally realized. A patronizing stance is likely to be bound up with issues of social privilege, norms, and fear of cultural and societal change more generally. And traditional and popular song texts can become the focal point for a wide variety of dissatisfactions and forms of nostalgia.

Of course there are counter-examples to the general point that the song texts tend to be repetitive, redundant, to rely on well-known forms, and to reflect familiar concerns. Many great poems have been set to music, and the best work of some songwriters can be compared without embarrassment to the work of poets who are their contemporaries. But while it is important to remember such exceptions and to be mindful of them in thinking about songs and singing more generally, these exceptions do not invalidate the general claims. I do not think that a "duel" between examples of banal and exceptional song texts will get us very far. The relatively low literary, aesthetic, and philosophical merit of many song texts simply underscores the facts that songs are *music* and texts are not. Hence evaluating the words of a song without reference to the music is to evaluate only part of a whole. It would be like judging a full-color painting on the basis of a black-and-white reproduction, or evaluating a film without reference to its soundtrack. While some limited judgments can be made in these kinds of cases, there is no way we could evaluate the whole work with any confidence.

Some Ontological Issues

Ontology is the branch of philosophy that examines the nature of existence and being. There are two main types of ontological questions we can ask about songs. First, what are a particular song's identity conditions. That is, what kind of changes can we make to a song and still maintain that it is the "same" song that we started with? Second, what manner of existence do songs have? Are they mental objects like ideas? Do they exist apart from their expression in performances and musical scores? Now we can ask ontological questions about anything in the world: the coffee cup on my desk, the Eiffel tower, the text of *War and Peace*, Beethoven's Ninth Symphony, Leonardo da Vinci's painting the *Mona Lisa*, the Rolling Stones' 1971 recording of "Brown Sugar" and so on.

Some of the objects on this list are generally considered to be artworks, and this status may or may not influence our thinking about their ontology. The ontology of art is a lively branch of philosophy with a variety of well-argued positions on offer. As with any philosophical question, before exploring ontological issues it is a good idea to first reflect upon our methodology and aspirations. What are we doing when we ask about the ontology of artworks and why are we doing it? What would a successful or plausible answer to an ontological question look like? So a few words about that before we go much further. Fortunately, there has been a good deal of reflection on these matters as well.

Amie Thomasson has written forcefully about the desiderata for an ontology of art. According to her view, answers to ontological questions about art are to be found in our practices or, more concretely, in the practices of those whose words and actions ground the terms.[4] Hence the ontological facts about artworks are not mind-independent. Instead they are determined by the grounders of art-terms. We learn about the ontology of the work of art through analysis of the concepts of those people who ground and reground the terms. So if we want to know about the ontology of songs we should pay attention to how singers, composers, songwriters, music producers, etc. use words like "song," "accompaniment," "cover version," and so on. Competent grounders cannot (as a whole) be massively ignorant of or in error about the ontological nature of the art kind they refer to, since their concepts are determinative of this. Philosophers can make slight adjustments in these conceptions – remove any seeming inconsistencies, make them more explicit, put them in a context – but that is all. Hence revisionary views about the ontology of art, if not false, are most charitably taken as proposals for how we might reform our existing practices.

A very different view of the ontology of art can be found in the work of Nelson Goodman.[5] Goodman is notorious in the philosophy of music for his counter-intuitive views about the identity conditions of musical works in performance. Goodman focused on notated works. Musical notation has two important qualities. First, it is finitely differentiated with respect to syntax. The shape and position of a note on the staff tells us its pitch and relative duration. In a neatly written score, we do not confuse one note for another, the way we might confuse a hand-written numeral "1" with a numeral "7." Second, musical notation is also finitely differentiated semantically. That is, a trained listener will be able to determine the symbol for a given musical tone and relative duration.

Goodman thought that these two qualities of musical notation held some serious implications for the identity conditions of musical works in performance. If a performance of a musical work departed in the smallest way from any of the notated features of its score, then that event, whatever its musical value and interest, did not count as a performance of that particular work. If one of the performers played a B flat when she should have played B natural, then the ensemble has not performed the work they intended to perform.

Critics were quick to point out that scores do not function in music in the way that Goodman seems to assume they do. Others rejected Goodman's position on the grounds that its implications were deeply implausible, not to say absurd. No one, listeners and musicians alike, accepts that one incorrect note is enough to disqualify a performance! Goodman had already anticipated some of these criticisms in *Languages of Art*:

> The practicing musician or composer usually bristles at the idea that a performance with one wrong note is not a performance of the given work at all; and ordinary usage surely sanctions overlooking a few wrong notes. But this is one of those cases where ordinary usage gets us quickly into trouble. The innocent-seeming principle that performances differing by just one note are instances of the same work risks the consequence – in view of the transitivity of identity – that all performances whatsoever are of the same work.[6]

Goodman was not out to reform everyday speech. If you insisted that the school band's error-ridden muddle through "The Star Spangled Banner" was a performance of that work, he would not correct you. Ordinary discourse is not philosophy, and certainly not ontology.

So we have two very different visions of methodology in the ontology of art. Thomasson, on the one hand, argues that the philosopher discovers facts about the identity conditions and manner of existence of artworks through a study of the concepts as they are employed by the grounders of the terms. Philosophers, in effect, defer to the community of those who ground the relevant terms, perhaps suggesting slight adjustments. Goodman, on the other hand, is comfortable with an ontology of art that may be at odds with the typical usage of the relevant concepts. Whatever the philosopher is doing when she works on the ontology of music, the conclusions she defends may be quite studiedly different from the presumptions of practicing musicians, composers, and others who ground the relevant terms. Her activities and their activities run on separate tracks, so to speak.

My own views on methodology reject both of these extremes. I disagree with Thomasson's (revisionary) proposal that the ontology of art is best conceived of as a project of conceptual analysis. In my view, Thomasson under estimates how radically the grounders of art-terms may disagree with one another. While we can point to certain established practices in the art world, other practices may not yet be established, they may vary from place to place, or they may be rapidly changing. Furthermore, the grounders' words and actions may not cohere. Uncovering the ontological assumptions behind our intuitions or behind some common artistic and critical practices, as Thomasson suggests that we do, is an important project (although I am not convinced that philosophers can do a good job of this without the help of social scientists). However, once these ontological assumptions have been uncovered, we should be open to the possibility that they might be mistaken in important respects.

I am also uncomfortable with Goodman's view of the philosopher's activity as grandly apart from the activity of those most concerned with the very subjects she is thinking about. Learning about how those who ground art-terms use them, the conceptual distinctions they make, the presumptions in their employment of terms, and the differences within the community of users, is potentially of great interest. Stephen Davies has suggested (sensibly, I think) that our ontology should be revealing of how and why art is created and appreciated.[7] One of the ways of making sure that it is so, is to pay attention to the discourse and the actions of those who ground the art-terms we are interested in investigating.

So I do not see the philosopher of art as deferring to those who ground the relevant terms (as Thomasson does), nor as removed from those who use the terms (as Goodman does), and certainly not as occupied in the correction of ordinary usage (as might be argued). Rather, I see the philosopher of art as engaged in a dialogue with those who ground the terms – with artists, musicians, composers, curators, music and art critics and fans, and so on. I hope that we might learn from one another. Artists and composers have long pushed against the conceptual boundaries of their disciplines, and the philosophy of art is enriched when it engages closely with art and with particular art works. I see the philosophy of art as offering an invitation to think more carefully or to think differently about some foundational issues, and in this way both philosophy and art might be enriched.

Accordingly, I favor a pragmatic approach to ontological issues. When considering, say, the ontological status of a song, I believe that we should first ask, "Who wants to know, and why?" A singer might have different reasons for asking than a music historian, a collector of folk songs, or an anthropologist. An intellectual property lawyer might, yet again, have different reasons. When people have different reasons for asking, it is not surprising if they all come up with different answers. Yet each may have good arguments for answering the question in a particular way, depending on their reasons for seeking to differentiate one song from another or to know a song's manner of existence.

In his book, *Musical Works and Performances,* Davies makes a useful distinction between ontologically "thick" and "thin" musical works. Thinner works determine less of the fine detail of their performance than do thicker ones.[8] Generally speaking, the thinner the work, the more interpretive freedom the musician is allowed, and the thinner the song text, the more acceptable it is to change the text in performance. A thick work gives musicians comparatively little freedom or room for interpretation. We have already seen that there is a continuum regarding the malleability of song texts, which seems to depend on genre and musical culture. The texts of traditional songs often allow performers a great deal of freedom; the texts of classical or "art" songs are thought to be less flexible.

Since, in this chapter, I have limited myself to talking about song texts rather than songs more generally, I will likewise focus here on problems raised by song texts. Even taking a thin song text and a "permissive" performance culture, there must be some point at which, if enough of the words are altered, we have not a version of the same song, but a different song. "John Brown's Body" and "The Battle Hymn of the Republic" are different songs, although both are sung to the tune of the spiritual "Canaan's Happy Shore." "The Bear Went Over the Mountain" and "For He's a Jolly Good Fellow" are different songs, despite sharing the same tune. So songs are, to some degree, differentiated by their texts. That is, a different text means a different song, even if the tune is the same.

What about changes to a song text that fall short of completely different words? Is "Happy Birthday to You" a different song each time it is sung because the name of the person addressed is changed? Considerations of ontological parsimony (the desire to admit the existence of only those entities that are necessary) lead me to say no. "Happy Birthday to You" is one song, not a different song each time it is sung. It belongs in a category of songs in which it is the convention to change certain words, depending on the occasion. In the case of "Happy Birthday to You," the name of the person addressed is changed. Similarly, rock songs that mention the name of a particular city are often altered in this way for live performances. The singer calls out the name of the city where he is performing, rather than calling out the name of the city in the song that was originally written and recorded.

Is "Happy Birthday" a different song than "Bonne Fête à toi" (which is sung at birthday parties in French Canada, to the same tune as "Happy Birthday to You")? I would argue that the answer to this question depends on who is asking it, and why. A singer in Montreal who is booked to sing at a birthday party needs to know if he is being asked for the English or the French version and he may treat them as different songs. A cultural anthropologist who is studying the practices of celebration in French and English Canada may be comfortable saying that both communities sing the "same" song at birthday parties.

Before leaving our initial look at the ontology of songs it is worth asking the question of what is to be gained by philosophical explorations of the ontology of music. If the singer, the music historian, the folk song collector, the anthropologist, and the intellectual property lawyer may legitimately answer the question differently, why even ask a philosopher as well? Aside from the fact that many philosophically minded people with an interest in music have been drawn to these questions, what might a philosophical perspective add to the other perspectives?

Aaron Ridley would likely say "not very much." Ridley has argued that serious philosophical engagement with music may be "impeded by" ontological speculation.[9] One of Ridley's main contentions is that metaphysical questions about musical works – their ontological status and identity conditions – are irrelevant ("absolutely worthless") if one's primary interests are aesthetic and evaluative. We do not ordinarily wonder if a performance has really been "of" a certain work. What we care about is whether the performance has been any good or not. Hence neutral, pre-theoretical thoughts about the ontology of music are enough. Further ontological speculation and specification will not do any evaluative work. If Ridley's arguments are sound, then they have serious consequences for the philosophy of music.

Ridley's critics have charged that, on the contrary, evaluative claims presuppose and require ontological commitments. As Andrew Kania has pointed out, perhaps Ridley in his article has helped himself a little too handily to "neutral pre-theoretical thoughts" and thereby smuggled in the ontological commitments that he needed for his arguments to get off the ground.[10] As much as he would like to, Ridley cannot avoid ontology any more than any philosopher of music

When I first read Ridley's arguments I found them bracing. He really pushed me to think about the whole project of musical ontology and why it might be worth one's time and effort. I am very suspicious of the claim (which, to be fair to Kania, he does not make) that we need to do ontology "before" we engage in further philosophical speculation, whether this claim is made of music, ethics, language, etc. While Kania may be correct that Ridley cannot avoid ontological commitments (and while philosophers of ethics, language, etc. also may not be able to avoid them), that is not the best way to frame this issue. Clearly, much good philosophical work has been done in a number of areas without the need for preliminary ontological speculation. For me, at least, the proper question to ask is whether philosophers of music should focus or concentrate on the metaphysics of music, perhaps to the detriment of attention to other kinds of questions. Does the ink spilt over musical ontology get us any closer to revealing how and why art is created and appreciated? How can we make sure that it does?

Unlike Ridley (and with Kania), I would argue that genuine ontological issues do indeed arise in the philosophy and aesthetics of music. I have discussed some of them already and will discuss more in the rest of the book. Ridley seems to want to limit the philosophy of music to "aesthetic and evaluative" questions. For him these are of the greatest interest, if not the sole interest. As he writes: "for unless one's philosophical engagement with music is driven by, and is of a sort that might pay dividends for, one's musical experience – including one's evaluative experience – there is no obvious sense in which one is engaged in philosophical *aesthetics* at all."[11] The problem with Ridley's claim, as I see it, is that we cannot decide *a priori* which questions and which lines of inquiry will "pay dividends for" musical enjoyment. We simply have to ask the questions, think through the issues, and see if this affects the way we attend to music or not. And while enriching one's musical enjoyment would certainly be one valuable outcome of philosophical and ontological inquiry about music, it is by no means the only possible valuable outcome.

What Singers Communicate

What is communicated or fails to be communicated through a song? I have already claimed that the presence of a text sets song apart from other types of music. So it might seem obvious that what singers communicate is song lyrics. Yet while singers do communicate words, that is not all they do. There is much more to be said.

First, not all musical traditions place value on exact communication of song texts. We have already seen that in many musical traditions singers are not expected to convey the exact words of a particular text in a fixed order. So conveying a song text, in at least some musical traditions, is not *necessary* for singing a particular song.

Is conveying a song text *sufficient* for singing a song? That is, if a singer succeeds in conveying lyrics, has he or she performed the song? The answer to this question is "yes" only if we accept that "performance" is a purely descriptive concept with no evaluative component. I reject this idea. Following other philosophers who have written on performance, I treat "performance" as an evaluative concept.[12] So not every act of singing a song counts as a performance of that song. (Later, in the chapter on performance, I will defend this understanding of performance more directly. It is vulnerable to some objections, but I believe that these can be answered.) A singer who sings a song in a manner that is flat, indifferent, or ill-suited to the song has not succeeded in performing it. So I would argue that conveying a song text is not sufficient for singing a song, if we take more than a bare or minimal notion of "singing."

Although singers communicate words, that is not all they do, nor all they are expected to do. Rather, singers use words, as well as other means, to communicate or share meaning. A discussion of song meaning will have to be put off until there is much more in place. Again, songs are music, not texts, and we cannot talk about song meaning while we limit ourselves to texts. I will need to discuss music as well as words, the act of singing, and the role of an audience before I can hope to give an adequate account of song meaning.

"House of the Rising Sun"

Before we proceed any further I need to make one thing clear. "House of the Rising Sun" was not written by the Animals. The song pre-dates their hit recording by many years. Some readers will wonder why I state the obvious. Yet if the comments on some of the many internet recordings are any indication, others will be hearing about this for the first time.

I was haunted by "House of the Rising Sun" long before I had any idea what it might be about. Eric Burdon's vocal performance is deeply evocative – surely one of the most arresting performances by a male lead vocalist in the rock tradition. (Sounds like the name of an award.) Although I was born after the Animals' recording became a hit, I remember hearing it often when I was growing up – on the radio, at the roller rink, and at school and community dances. I admit that the Animals' recording is so firmly implanted in my mind that it is difficult for me not to compare other recordings to it (although it is no longer my favorite). Eric Burden sings with total conviction. I now realize that there is something a little bizarre or uncanny about the assurance with which he sings in the final verse about "Going back to New Orleans ... ." Eric Burden had barely left the U.K. in 1964.

I heard this song – in the Animals' recording and in many others – before I thought very much about what it was about. Indeed, I'm still not sure what it is about. Is the narrator a man or a woman? What is the "house of the rising sun" – a prison, a brothel, an asylum, or something else?

Historians of folk music trace the song's origins to England. It is one of many songs that crossed the Atlantic with British emigrants and was re-imagined in its new home. There are many different versions, as you would expect of a traditional song. In some versions the narrator is a man, and in some it is a woman. (Male singers have recorded the female version.) Other versions, found by folk music collectors, are sexually explicit and warn the listener about the danger of sexually transmitted diseases. The version that most of us are familiar with (whether sung by the Animals, by Nina Simone, or by Bob Dylan) is based on Alan Lomax's publication of the text in *Our Singing Country* in 1941. Lomax in turn based his composite version on a couple of field recordings that he collected in Eastern Kentucky in 1937. The version on which he relied most heavily was sung by a teenage girl named Georgia Turner.

"House of the Rising Sun" is in some ways a typical traditional song, and in other ways less so. It bears several marks of oral communication. The text is simple, with elements of redundancy. The patterns of rhyme would have helped singers to remember the lyrics. There is less repetition than we might expect in a traditional song, although this may be because older versions of the song have been lost. The malleability of its lyrics (and, as we will see later, of the music) are characteristic of traditional songs. Its theme of regret ("If I had only listened to what my Mama said") is traditional, and these exact words express regret in other traditional songs. We also find the admonition to warn a younger sibling ("Go tell my baby sister," "Tell my youngest brother") in other traditional songs. Yet other sections of the lyrics have not been found (at least not to date) in other places. For example, the line in the penultimate verse about "One foot on the platform and one foot on the train" seems to be unique to this song.

Thematically, "House of the Rising Sun" reflects concerns that would have been relevant to many in the community. We can find similar themes in many other British and American traditional songs, in similar or different words: the father (or sweetheart) who is a "rambler" or a gambler or a drunkard; the regret over mistakes made and sorrow about what one's life has become. Yet some aspects of the song make it distinctively American. Most obviously, the reference to "New Orleans" and the reference to a train. In 1937, when Lomax visited Eastern Kentucky, the railroad had been an agent of social change for at least a generation and had ended decades of isolation. The train represented freedom of mobility and the chance to seek opportunities and remake one's life elsewhere. It also represented danger and temptation to young people, epitomized by one of the rail's endpoints: New Orleans. Ted Anthony, in his book *Chasing the Rising Sun: The Journey of an American Song*, puts this well: "New Orleans was a particular object of attraction and suspicion, and the railroad's arrival in Appalachia only accentuated that. It almost defied belief that the tracks that came through your very own little mountain town could be connection with that place *down there*."[13]

My decision to begin with song texts apart from music must break down here. Without considering the music and the tune to which "House of the Rising Sun" is sung, I cannot say much more about it. Some of the versions with very different lyrics have been sung to similar tunes. And to make things more complicated, different tunes have underpinned the same (or highly similar) lyrics. As we found in the more general discussion of ontology, if we are interested in the ontology of a *song* as opposed to a song *text*, then we have to consider both words and music. And if we want to understand what a singer communicates in singing a song, beyond generalities, we have to think not only about words and music, but about other aspects of performance and about audiences as well.

So let's talk about music.

Notes

1 See James Reeves, *The Idiom of the People: English Traditional Verse from the MSS of Cecil Sharp* (London: Mercury Books, 1961).
2 Keith Richards, *Life* (New York: Little, Brown & Co., 2010), 277.
3 Reeves, *The Idiom of the People*, 1–4.
4 Amie Thomasson, "The Ontology of Art and Knowledge in Aesthetics," *Journal of Aesthetics and Art Criticism* 63:3 (2005), 221–29. I also benefited from hearing a critique of Thomasson's views presented by Thomas Adajian at the American Society for Aesthetics Eastern Division Meeting in 2006.
5 Nelson Goodman, *Languages of Art* (Indianapolis: Hackett Publishing Co., 1976), Chapters 4 and 5.
6 Goodman, *Languages,* 186.
7 Stephen Davies, "Ontology of Art," in Jerrold Levinson (ed.), *The Oxford Handbook of Aesthetics* (Oxford: Oxford University Press, 2003), 155–80.
8 See Stephen Davies, *Musical Works and Performances: A Philosophical Exploration* (Oxford: Clarendon Press, 2001), 3–4.
9 Aaron Ridley, "Against Musical Ontology," *Journal of Philosophy* 100:4 (2003), 203.
10 Andrew Kania, "Piece for the End of Time: In Defense of Musical Ontology," *British Journal of Aesthetics* 48:1 (2008), 65–79.
11 Ridley, "Against Musical Ontology," 208.
12 See Stan Godlovitch, *Musical Performance* (London: Routledge, 1998) and Paul Thom, *For an Audience* (Philadelphia: Temple, 1993).
13 Ted Anthony, *Chasing the Rising Sun* (New York: Simon & Schuster, 2007), 19. Italics in the original. I have relied on this book for much of the information on the history of "House of the Rising Sun."

2   Music and Words

When I told a musical friend that I planned to use "House of the Rising Sun" as a central example in a book on song and singing, and that I thought that much of the song's appeal could be attributed to its text, she was skeptical. In her view, the success of the Animals' hit recording could be traced to its minor key tonality and unusual (for rock music) triple meter. "Think of it in a major key and duple meter and who cares about the words then?" she challenged me.

Same Words, Different Music

When we talk about the "music" of a song we might mean one of several things. Most obviously, there is the melody or tune to which the words are sung. In a cappella (unaccompanied) singing, this is as far as it goes. However, most of the time we can also think about the relationship between the vocal line of a song and its instrumental accompaniment. In much art music, such as Schubert's lieder, a song's accompaniment is stable and notated in a score. Performers are permitted interpretive choices only within a small scope. In other musical genres, especially those that have roots in folk music (including rock, jazz, and country), performers have a good deal more freedom and can vary the accompaniment greatly, including varying the musical arrangement and the instrumentation.

"House of the Rising Sun" provides some ready illustrations of interpretive freedom and choice. As the song moved from a folk song sung by ordinary people to material for professional performance and recording, singers and musicians arranged the song in different ways. Early Appalachian performers, The Callahan Brothers and Ashley and Foster, accompanied the song with strumming acoustic guitars. Esco Hankins sang it against the background of a string band in 1947. Nina Simone recorded it live at least twice: a slow, meditative take with a very spare jazz backing at the Village Gate in 1962 and a later, up-tempo version with a larger ensemble at the Montreux Jazz Festival in 1968. And surely some of the appeal of the Animals' hit recording can be traced to the interplay between the vocal line and the pulsating organ chords and to the now-famous opening electric guitar A-minor arpeggio.

When my friend challenged me on "House of the Rising Sun," I doubt that she realized that the song had indeed been performed and recorded in duple meter (with the accent on every second beat rather than on every third) and in a major key. And I have to concede that she was on to something. The song sounds very different when sung in this way. If someone's first exposure to the song was through one of the duple-meter, major-tonality versions, they might not be drawn to the words enough to reflect on them.

To understand the difference that meter and tonality can make, we need only to compare two pre-Animals versions of "House of the Rising Sun." Woody Guthrie recorded the song in 1941.[1] He sings and strums the guitar in cut time (duple meter) in major key tonality with few chord changes. Guthrie sings without much affect, and the simple guitar accompaniment chiming along makes the song sound upbeat, especially if you get caught up in the rhythm rather than attend to the words. If you know the words and understand their theme of remembrance and regret, Guthrie's almost jaunty take sounds incongruous. The words and music simply do not suit one another; they seem to express different things. If this was the first version of the song that I had heard, I doubt that I would have been impressed with the song or sought out other renditions.

Compare Guthrie's treatment with the performance by Josh White, an African-American singer whose career began on "race" records marketed to African-Americans. White recorded "House of the Rising Sun" in 1947.[2] Like Guthrie, he accompanies himself on the guitar, but rather than strumming chords his fingers pluck out a delicate accompanying melody. He sings and plays in a minor key and in a slow triple meter. The overall effect is bluesy and meditative. White's performance draws our attention to the words of the song. Even if we know the song well, he makes us want to hear what is coming next. The minor key vocal line and graceful accompanying melody seem to go together perfectly with the sentiments expressed in the lyrics and all three make up a consistently expressive whole.

In fact, the performances by Guthrie and White are so different that, when I urged my friend to listen to Guthrie's version, her response was that Guthrie was not actually performing "House of the Rising Sun." She told me, "The words are the same, but changed harmonic structure, melody, time signature, KEY. There's a breaking point and I can't define it but I know it when I hear it. This is Woody Guthrie's song 'X,' with words from 'House of the Rising Sun.'" In her view, the musical differences between what Guthrie sings and the song she thought she knew had clear ontological implications: rather than two contrasting versions of the same song, we should really be talking about two different songs.

Some Ontological Issues (Continued)

My friend raised a valid point. What kind of changes can we make to the music of a song and still maintain that it is the "same" song that we started with? I argued in the previous chapter for a pragmatic approach to ontological issues when it came to the words of a song, and I would argue for a similarly pragmatic approach to a song's musical component. When considering the identity conditions of a song – what needs to obtain for a performance to count as being of a specific song – I believe that we should first ask, "Who wants to know, and why?" Different interested parties may have good reasons for answering the question in different ways.

"House of the Rising Sun" is a "thin" rather than a "thick" work; that is, performers are permitted a good deal of interpretive freedom. They can make a variety of musical choices and still be playing the same song as others who have made different choices. But how thin is the song? There must be a point at which it is plausible to say that a performer has not performed "House of the Rising Sun" but a different, perhaps related, work. To be sure, folk songs can change so much over time that their identity conditions are violated and we end up with different songs. The traditional ballad "The Unfortunate Rake" is a good example. In the earliest versions of this song, the narrator meets a fellow soldier who is dying of syphilis. The song has evolved over time into a number of variants with similar thematic content, including "The Streets of Laredo" and "The St. James Infirmary Blues." Few would argue, I think, that these three songs are really "the same" despite their common origin.

Does Guthrie's performance reach the point that he is singing a song other than "House of the Rising Sun"? I would say no. To my mind, he is singing a version or variation of "House" rather than a different song. The commonalities shared by Guthrie's lyrics and by other performances of the song provide us with a path back into its history. Guthrie was not the only performer to record "House" in a major key; Roy Acuff (the "King of Country Music") and the duo Ashley and Foster also did. All of these early performers presumably learned the song from an earlier source, and perhaps these can be traced back to common sources. So there is a tradition of singing the song in this way.

Treating these major and minor key versions as being of "the same" song allows us to ask questions about the song's trajectory across time and the ways in which different communities have changed it. It also allows us to evaluate Guthrie's performance against other performances of "House of the Rising Sun." If he and White are singing different songs, then we can make only limited comparisons between them. It would be problematic to say that White's version is aesthetically better than Guthrie's because we would be comparing apples with oranges.

Music and Words Together

It is clear that setting words to different tunes, or even the "same" tune in a different musical modality, can make us hear those words differently. Taking the same melody and using different instrumentation or a different musical arrangement can also make a difference to our perception of the words and to the overall musical experience. Although both play the guitar, Guthrie's rhythmic strummed chords frame "House of the Rising Sun" very differently than does White's fingered melody. Music can reinforce the meaning of a song's lyrics, as when a sad-sounding melody accompanies lyrics imbued with remorse or heartbreak. Or music can elide the meaning of a song's words, when what is expressed by the music seems in contrast to what is expressed by the words. An expressive contrast between words and music need not be an aesthetic failure. A divergence between the meaning of the words and the expressive character of the music might reinforce the impact of words or music, or it might be heard as ironic, or it might make us question what we thought we had understood, either about the words or about the music.

Many different kinds of relationships can obtain between words and music, and different relationships will have different implications for listeners. What can we say more generally about the relationship between the words and music of a song, and what can this tell us about the experience of listening to vocal music?

The dominant philosophical view on this question (more often assumed than explicitly articulated) is that songs are hybrids or fusions of words and music. Aaron Ridley is surely right to claim that this way of thinking about song is "hugely well-entrenched."[3]

Thinking of songs as compounds made up of words and music has an intuitive rightness. It seems natural to think of a song as a hybrid combining words and music which are composed separately and then brought together, or to think of a composer being handed a text and told to set it to music. It seems natural because the words and music of a song seem to be easily separated. They are even notated in different ways. We can take the words of a song and put them to different music, or we can take the music of a song and sing different words. The early folk song collectors I mentioned in the first chapter sometimes notated the music of a song but could not be bothered to write down the words. They treated the words and music of songs as separable entities.

Indeed, the hybrid model seems correct because we know of many songs that came into being when a previously written text was set to music. But it would be mistaken to think that all songs began in such a way, or that all songs are best understood in such a way. Despite its intuitive appeal and despite the fact that many songs do indeed come into being when a text is set to music, the hybrid model is an inadequate account of songs generally and accepting it skews our appreciation of songs in unfortunate ways. Let me explain.

The most philosophically rich account of hybrid art forms is that of Jerrold Levinson. For Levinson, the key difference between a "hybrid" art form (such as opera or collage) and a "non-hybrid" (such as instrumental music or painting) is that the antecedents of hybrid art forms are still evident in them and should be taken into account in our responses. Opera, for example, is recognizable as a combination of drama and music and an appropriate response takes both into account.[4] There would be something a little perverse in attending an opera and ignoring much of the dramatic aspect by keeping your eyes closed throughout the performance, while there would be nothing amiss in doing so at a concert of (non-hybrid) instrumental music. (Although we will see, by the time we reach Chapter 8 on music drama, that not everyone agrees.)

Hybrid models of song are historically uninformed. There is no evidence that the earliest songs were hybrid forms, with pre-existing texts set to music. Strictly speaking we cannot even be sure that language originated before music or that speaking came before singing. A number of thinkers, including some contemporary researchers, have argued that music originated before language or that the two have a common origin.[5] According to the best evidence we have, music and poetry were unified in earliest times. Their separation – what has been called music's "emancipation" from language – came later.[6] And since purely instrumental music arises out of vocal music – not the other way around – we cannot make claims about what constitutes an "appropriate" response based on vocal music's supposed origins as a hybrid form.

Turning to specific songs, rather than songs in general, the genesis of many songs is simply lost in time. We do not know where the words of "House of the Rising Sun" came from, only that its overall themes and some of its lyrics can be found in earlier songs. Nor do we know how those words came to be connected with the melody we are now familiar with. To be fair to Levinson, he makes a distinction between traditional songs (which he does not think of as hybrids) and other kinds of songs.[7] While Levinson's distinction shows sensitivity to the differences between songs, accepting the hybrid model for non-traditional songs would mean two fundamentally different approaches to song. Traditional and non-traditional songs would be as different from one another are as painting and collage, with possibly different implications for performers and audiences. This seems a high price to pay for keeping the hybrid model for some songs, especially when audiences often cannot always easily determine whether they are listening to a traditional song or one that was composed more recently. And this difficulty in telling the difference between traditional and non-traditional songs is not only a function of listeners' lack of familiarity with musical genres. Composers as different as Bob Dylan and Franz Schubert have composed songs with the intention of making them sound like "found" folk music.

The idea that songs are best thought of as combinations of pre-existing texts and suitable melodies is at odds with some of the things we know about how at least some non-traditional songs come to be written. Keith Richards' autobiography offers one perspective on the creative process of songwriting. He recounts something quite different to setting a pre-existing text to music. Typically, Richards would work out a chord structure or sound patterns on the guitar, and then he and Mick Jagger would work together to find words to fit the sound, with Jagger bearing primary responsibility for the lyrics. For example, he writes of their song "Salt of the Earth": "I think I came up with the title of that and had the basic spur of it, but Mick did all the verses. This was our thing. I'd spark the idea, 'Let's drink to the hardworking people, let's drink to the salt of the earth,' and after that, Mick, it's all yours. Halfway through he'd say, where do we break it? Where do we go to the middle? Where's the bridge?"[8]

The genesis of "Jumpin' Jack Flash" provides another illustration. Richards recalls that he and Jagger had been up nearly all night, and at dawn Jagger was woken by the sound of heavy stomping rubber boots near the window. The boots belonged to Richards' gardener Jack Dyer. When Jagger asked, "What's that?" Richards replied "Oh that's Jack. That's jumping Jack." Then, he tells us, "I started to work around the phrase on the guitar, which was in open tuning, singing the phrase 'Jumping Jack.' Mick said 'Flash' and suddenly we had this phrase with a great rhythm and ring to it. So we got to work on it and wrote it."[9]

Richards' remarks are a good reminder that language has musical qualities. Words have a musical aspect even when they are not sung or set to music. The musical qualities of language can be enhanced or weakened when groups of words are put together in different ways. Notice what Richards says about the words he and Jagger came upon for "Jumpin' Jack Flash": They had a "great rhythm and ring." He is keenly attuned to the musical elements of the emerging lyrics. And as Jagger writes the song text, he is attuned to musical structure – where to "break" the song and go to the bridge. Words are valued for their musical qualities and arranged with attention to musical structure.

Peter Kivy has made a similar point about the way that music and words work together in a different musical genre. He writes that we cannot take, for example, a Renaissance motet and say, "'this is what the music does, and this is what the words do, and by consequence, this is what the words and music do together.' *That cannot be how the composers thought.*"[10] Indeed, for all the differences between them, Renaissance composers probably thought in ways not that different from how Richards and Jagger think when they are composing, allowing for the variances in musical genre, historical epoch, and self-perception.

What about the songs that we know to have been composed when a pre-existing text was set to music? Does the hybrid model not fit them? I would argue that even when a composer is handed a text and asked to set it to music, the hybrid model limits our understanding of the nature of songs. Ridley has written at length about the relationship between music and words in songs and I am indebted to his work. He reminds us that the sound qualities of words as sung are likely to be different from the qualities of those same words as spoken, as different syllables are articulated and rhythms used to guide listeners' attention in specific ways. So the words "as such" (spoken or read silently) are not the same as the words when set to music and sung. They have different sound qualities, they work together in different ways, and they have different (sometimes heightened) expressive properties. Martin Boykan put it well when he said that language undergoes a "sea change" as soon as music is added.[11]

If the hybrid model will not do, how should we think about songs? What kind of thing is a song? Following Ridley, I regard song as a distinct musical form that contains words or some other kind of vocal component.[12] Consequently a poem set to music is best thought of as a new work of art that uses the same words as the poem.[13]

Judging Songs

Thinking of songs as hybrids has a number of unfortunate implications for our evaluative practices.

Because hybrid models encourage us to think of works in terms of, and in light of, their components, they can support a bias against songs whose texts are not self-standing; that is, whose texts do not work simply as spoken or as read silently from the page. I note the longevity of a particular kind of mockery, when an actor or comedian does a "straight" recital of popular song (or now rap) lyrics that were clearly meant to be sung or at least articulated against a musical background. The idea is to draw attention to the words without the "distraction" of music and allow audiences to recognize their triviality or salacious undertones. This practice was thought to be funny (and indeed could be funny) on the late-night TV of my youth, and continues to inspire professional comedians and aspiring amateurs on the internet. Yet mocking or criticizing the words of a song for not working as poetry is misguided. It is as misguided as expecting to dance along to a poetry recital. In most cases, the words of a song are simply not meant to stand alone, any more than the color of a painting is meant to stand apart from its design. In the few cases where song lyrics can work as poetry (as in the songs of Cole Porter, for example), that is cause for high praise, not a reason to deride those songs whose lyrics fail to reach that standard.

The hybrid model seems not to be applicable to those songs whose vocal component is not text-based. This includes vocal practices as different as vocalise (singing a vowel sound rather than words), doo-wop, and scat singing. Most seriously, if we judge songs as combinations of words and music, then our primary interest is likely to turn on how well the music fits the words. A song is seen to be successful if music does good service to words. As Boykan puts it, vocal music is discussed, "as though it were some sort of exercise in literary criticism"[14] rather than an activity with a *musical* focus. In effect the words are seen as more important than music.

Levinson's influential account of the relationship between words and music falls into this trap. According to Levinson, our main evaluative question about a song should be how aesthetically good a compound do the words and music make. When we evaluate a song, Levinson writes, a number of questions are relevant, including how well the expressiveness of the music matches the emotional tone of the text, and how well the music of the song conforms to the "natural music" of the text. He proposes that the ideal comportment between music and words is one of "mutual suitability" or "holistic working," rather than internal matching or mirroring. He compares the relationship between words and music in a good song to that of a (happily) married couple, whose interaction with one another is mutually rewarding.[15]

Levinson's talk of "conformity" or "mutual suitability" within a song presumes that there is one thing to suit or conform to another. But we have already seen that songs are best thought of not as compounds or hybrids, but as self-standing wholes. At first glance, it seems that Levinson puts words and music on equal footing. (I assume that such is one implication of his analogy between successful songs and happy marriages.) Yet since he assumes the hybrid model (with words and music as distinct antecedents) and since the examples he discusses are poems set to music, it is clear that the *music* is meant to match and conform to the text, not the other way around. Music is in service to the words.

Even Ridley – who writes so perceptively about song and singing – veers close to writing about vocal music as a form of literary criticism when he tries to improve upon existing accounts. For him, the best setting of a text to music is not one that "matches" the text in some way but rather one that shows that the composer has understood the text in question.[16] Drawing on the work of Ludwig Wittgenstein, Ridley distinguishes between "external" and "internal" understanding. We show that we have an external understanding of a phrase when we can paraphrase it; that is, when we can say the same thing in different words. So "Bake the pie for about 30 minutes" and "Put the pie in the heated oven for about half an hour" have equivalent meanings and one way of showing that we understand the first phrase would be to pronounce the second, and vice versa. But art is different – here an "internal" understanding is also relevant, and we indicate an internal understanding when we understand that what is expressed could be expressed only by *those* words in *that* order. The meaning of the opening phrase of T.S. Eliot's "The Waste Land" simply could not be expressed adequately by words other than "April is the cruelest month." If someone believes "The fourth month of the year is really nasty" to be an equivalent paraphrase, then she has simply not understood the poem as a poem. She may have understood the literal meaning of the words – since she has offered a phrase that is roughly equivalent in meaning – but there is more to understanding a poem than grasping the literal meaning.

With the distinction between external and internal understanding in place, Ridley argues that the best setting of a text to music is one that shows that the composer has understood the text in question. Specifically, the composer shows her internal understanding of a text by setting it to music in such a way that it is transformed into one text rather than another. (Keep in mind that although a poem and a song may share the same words, the addition of music transforms the song into a different text, with different sound qualities, different patterns of emphasis, possibly a different rhythm, different emotional resonances, and perhaps a different meaning.)

One strength of Ridley's proposal is that the song is evaluated as a whole. There is no talk of "matching" one thing to another or the "appropriateness" of one medium to another. And I have to agree with Ridley that some song settings make me wonder whether the composer really did understand the text. But this emphasis on understanding text makes song composition a variety of literary criticism. A poor composer may comprehend both the literal meaning of the words (external understanding) and understand why just those words in that order are essential (internal understanding). Yet he may be unable to show that understanding by setting the words to a suitable tune. Similarly, the fact that a composer has written a gorgeous melody does not, to my mind, show that he has understood the text he has set. If the text is banal then there would be no way to judge the composer's understanding of it through the beautiful music he has composed. Yet a beautiful setting of banal words is hardly some kind of failure. I doubt that we would want the composer to write a banal tune rather than something musically interesting. The successful composer does something *musical*. The evaluation of a song should not be an exercise in judging whether or not the composer understood the text.

How then to evaluate songs as songs, rather than as proxies for the understanding of a text? What counts as a good song? Can we still talk about successful or appropriate settings of texts without veering into literary criticism?

I think that the answer to these questions hinges on what words and music do for one another, and that is not a simple question to answer. The best short answer I know to this question is that words in songs may be "reinforced, accented, blurred, inspired to a new meaning, in a continual interplay" by accompanying music.[17] In other words, music (and performers' interpretations of that music) can do a lot. Being "appropriate" or not is just one kind of relation that music can have to words, and showing their understanding of those words is just one thing that composers can do.

In my view, a good song (words and music) is one that provides listeners with a good experience. One way a song might do this is by having a matching or "appropriate" relationship between words and music, but such a relationship is no guarantee of a song's aesthetic value. A tune can be appropriate to words but musically uninteresting. A tune can be inappropriate to the words but win us over nonetheless. A mismatch between words and music – or music that makes us wonder whether the composer understood the words – constitutes an aesthetic failure when the experience it provides listeners is poor. This can happen if the music and words are incongruous yet there is no compensating aesthetic payoff. Songwriting is a form of music writing, and the words of the song are part of its music. However difficult it is to specify how the two work well together and why, the answer is not to treat the words as dominant in a hybrid pair.

"Dover Beach"

"Dover Beach" is a poem by Matthew Arnold (1822–88) set to music by the American composer Samuel Barber (1910–81). Unlike the folk and rock music that I have been taking as examples, it is a "thick" work. The vocalist and instrumentalists (a string quartet) are expected to stick closely to the score. Needless to say, the singer should not take liberties with Arnold's text.[18] What can we say about how the words and music of "Dover Beach" work together and influence one another, and how should these factors influence our judgment of the song?

The poem is melancholy and pessimistic. Small wonder that this tissue of errors accompanies one of the many videos of the song available on the internet:

> This brooding song for baritone and string quartet, written in the days preceding World War II, might be taken as an attempt to warn, for it sets with almost miraculous appropriateness one of the grimmest poems of World War I.
>
> (All Music Guide)[19]

Barber wrote the song in 1931 – hardly "in the days" preceding World War II. And Arnold was dead long before the outbreak of World War I in 1914. I find these errors interesting, as they reveal a truth about the poem and the song. While the unknown author's chronology is off, there is indeed something admonitory and forbidding in both the poem and the song, an impression which is enhanced by the mysterious and violent image that closes the poem: of ignorant armies who "clash by night." The armies are "ignorant" because the soldiers cannot see one another in the darkness. According to Ian Hamilton, the reference is to a passage in Thucydides. During the night-time battle of Epipolae (part of the Peloponnesian War) the two sides were unable to distinguish one another and some soldiers may have been killed in error by their own comrades.[20] So the poem and song end with a powerful image of the futility of war.

The poem as a whole sets up a contract between vision and hearing. It begins with the poet gazing out of the window at the sea. The beauty and calm of the sea and the sweetness of the night air are belied by the "note of sadness" in the sound of pebbles being flung up the strand. The auditory imagery continues throughout; much of the poem is about sound. The sound of the pebbles connects us with the Classical past, as Sophocles heard the same "tremulous cadence" on the Aegean. The "retreat of faith," a preoccupation of Arnold's Victorian era, is symbolized by a "melancholy withdrawing roar." With this wealth of auditory imagery it is easy to see why Barber thought "Dover Beach" a suitable song text, despite its irregular structure and lack of a regular rhyme scheme.

The contrast between vision and hearing is only one of the tensions or oppositions in the poem. The sea is itself is an ambiguous subject. The opening lines describe the sea's beauty and stillness. But the sea is also a source of danger and a place of death, as Arnold would have expected his readers to recognize. In the first stanza a contrast is set up between the "cliffs" of England and the "coast" of France. The light on the French coast (surely a reference to the French Enlightenment) "gleams and is gone." I have already mentioned the tension between the present (as the poet now beckons us to the window) and the past, which is invoked by the image of the dramatist Sophocles likewise hearing the sound of the sea. That sound reminds Sophocles of the "ebb and flow" of human misery – another image of opposition. The final stanza contains the poem's most searing contrast, between the way the world seems ("so various, so beautiful, so new") and the way the world actually is (without joy, love, light, certitude, peace, or help for pain).

So far I have spoken about the poem and not the song. The melody is lyrical and slow enough that the singer can enunciate each word clearly. In some places, Barber's music seems to illustrate Arnold's text, as when the words "tremulous cadence" are set to an up-and-down musical figure that suggests, well, a tremulous cadence. Yet in other places Barber's music seems almost to stand in opposition to Arnold's text. For example, the song begins with the strings playing an uneasy back-and-forth rhythm. Then the singer enters.

The sea is calm tonight

From the very beginning the words and music seem to pull in different directions. The lyrics tell us that the sea is tranquil but the accompanying melody says something else. The melody of the opening lyric and the singer's words seem to be pulling in a different direction from the accompanying strings. Are they working against each other and does their opposition mar the song? To my ear, the opposition between the vocal line and the accompaniment is highly appropriate. It exemplifies and draws our attention to the tensions in the poem that I mentioned earlier: between the visual and the auditory, between the beauty and danger of the sea, and between the way the world seems and the way it is.

Although I was familiar with the poem before I heard the song, I no longer read the poem in the way that I used to. Knowing the song, and the particular way that Barber's music shapes the phrases and emphasizes particular words within them, makes me read the poem differently. My attention is focused in different ways. One example is in the words which open the final and most pessimistic stanza:

Ah, love, let us be true
To one another!

Before I heard the song, I read these words as a kind of plea. (Arnold's biographers speculate that Arnold wrote the poem around the time of his honeymoon – some of which was spent in Dover – and is addressing his bride.)[21] Yet in Barber's composition these words are sung to a crescendo and are also preceded by a crescendo in the strings. To me this makes them sound more like a demand or a challenge than like a plea. Now, Barber is a composer of great skill and could have set these words differently, making them sound like an appeal or an ultimatum or a wish. These different possibilities are just some of the various interpretive and musical choices he could have made. The proper way to judge the success of his choice is to ask how it works within the context of the rest of the song and what kind of an experience it can give listeners. Comparing the words in the poem with the words as sung does not really illuminate the musical choices Barber made, given that he could have made different (presumably equally appropriate) choices. Speculating about Barber's understanding of the words is similarly unfruitful. The fact that he sets them to sound like a demand or challenge does not necessarily indicate that he understood them in that way and only in that way. The point is not Barber's understanding of the poem but how the words and music work within the overall context of the song. And to answer that question we must appeal to listeners' experience.

Barber was a trained singer as well as a composer and he recorded "Dover Beach" with the Curtis String Quartet in 1937. I said, at the end of Chapter 1, that to focus on the song texts without considering music was very limiting. I could not say very much about songs without discussing words and music together. Having now expanded the discussion to music and words, I find that judging a song means understanding something about the experience it can offer listeners. But listeners can experience songs (and other music) only through performance. While it is true that some people can read a score and "hear" music in their minds, this is a form of imagining sound rather than actually experiencing it. So the time has come to consider song performance. What do singers do?

Notes

1 Available at http://youtu.be/UlbLs_bvimU (accessed December 9, 2014).
2 Available at http://youtu.be/ETOiPn_wK1s (accessed December 9, 2014).
3 Aaron Ridley, *The Philosophy of Music: Theme and Variations* (Edinburgh: Edinburgh University Press, 2004), 79.
4 Jerrold Levinson, "Hybrid Art Forms," in *Music, Art, & Metaphysics: Essays in Philosophical Aesthetics* (Ithaca: Cornell University Press, 1990), 30.
5 See for example Steven Mithen, *The Singing Neanderthals: The Origins of Music, Language, Mind, and Body* (Cambridge, MA: Harvard University Press, 2006).
6 John Neubauer, *The Emancipation of Music from Language: Departure from Mimesis in Eighteenth-Century Aesthetics* (New Haven: Yale University Press, 1986).

7 Levinson, "Hybrid Art Forms," 29.

8 Richards, *Life*, 237.

9 Richards, *Life*, 241.

10 Peter Kivy, *New Essays on Musical Understanding* (Oxford: Clarendon Press, 2001), 172 (emphasis added).

11 Martin Boykan, "Reflections on Words and Music," *The Musical Quarterly* 84:1 (2000), 135.

12 Again, Ridley argues this point forcefully.

13 Boykan, "Reflections," 124.

14 Boykan, "Reflections," 123.

15 Levinson, "Song and Music Drama," in *The Pleasures of Aesthetics* (Ithaca: Cornell University Press, 1996), 48–50.

16 Ridley, *The Philosophy of Music*, 97–98.

17 Mark W. Booth, *The Experience of Songs* (New Haven: Yale University Press, 1981), 8.

18 The text of the poem can be found here: www.victorianweb.org/authors/arnold/writings/doverbeach.html (accessed December 9, 2014).

19 See http://youtu.be/BmO7qX0-qu4 (accessed December 9, 2014). The video is no longer available but the text remains.

20 Ian Hamilton, *A Gift Imprisoned: The Poetic Life of Matthew Arnold* (London: Bloomsbury Publishing Co., 1998), 144–45.

21 Julia Touche, "The Biographical Contexts of 'Dover Beach' and 'Calais Sands': Matthew Arnold in 1851," The Victorian Web, www.victorianweb.org/authors/arnold/touche2.html (accessed December 9, 2014).

3   Giving Voice (What Do Singers Do?)

> Because music is always written for an audience. It is not written for a
> museum or for the composer himself.
>
> (Christoph Prégardien, tenor)[1]

What do singers do? It seems like an obvious question. Singing is a physical
activity. Singers move breath over the larynx and shape the resulting sound
into consonants and vowels with their tongue, teeth, and lips. Yet singing is
at the same time a social and cultural activity, and some singing is an art
form. Singers do something bodily, but they also do something that is subject to a variety of collective expectations and takes place within specific
shared contexts. What a singer does when he or she sings will depend
heavily on social and cultural factors, and on the expectations of both the
singer and those in attendance.

To see how this might be so, consider the differences between singing and
speech. Using a spectrograph, George List recorded the pitch contours of
various vocal activities and found many gradations between everyday speech
and singing. Speech intonation may level out and approach a monotone or
be heightened and exaggerated.[2] Examples of vocal communication that fall
sonically between singing and speech, yet arguably belong clearly to neither
include singspiel, recitative, rap, children's skipping and clapping rhymes,
auctioneers' chants, street sellers' calls and cries, field and street hollers, the
chants used in meditation and religious practices, and calls to prayer. So the
distinction between singing and speech is not purely physiological; instead, it
is best made along cultural and pragmatic grounds.

Whether any of the practices I've just mentioned are considered examples
of "song" (or indeed examples of music) depends on cultural expectations
and related attitudes regarding these very categories. For example, in cultures where music is understood as a secular pursuit, participants may be
reluctant to describe their vocal activity as singing and prefer to define it
as part of a larger spiritual practice. Islamic calls to prayer may sometimes
sound like songs but are not usually considered to be singing performances.
Similarly, the role of the cantor or chazzan in Judaism is seen to be primarily moral or spiritual rather than musical. Where music and singing have

little cultural prestige, musicians and singers may prefer to re-describe their musical activity as something else. ("I'm not a musician. I only play at weddings," memorably reported one informant in an article I once read by a sociolinguist who specialized in Arabic.)[3]

A Taxonomy of Song

A good place to start thinking about what singers do is to think about different kinds of songs. Given the ubiquity of songs the world over, there are many different types of songs, sung in many different contexts and serving diverse purposes. A philosophical approach appropriate for thinking about one type of song and singing may not be fruitful when applied to another type of song.

The composer Edward Cone proposed a classification of songs based partially on musical and partially on functional considerations. "Simple songs" have no accompaniment or only simple accompaniment.[4] An "art song" is a poem set to a composed vocal line and united with a fully developed instrumental accompaniment. (An example is Barber's setting of Arnold's "Dover Beach," which we discussed in the previous chapter). In contrast to art songs are "natural songs" such as ballads, in which the roles of the poet and composer are "hardly relevant."[5] Cone's "natural songs" would seem to overlap more-or-less with what I have called traditional songs. Finally "functional songs" are a variety of natural songs. In them, the singer does not "perform" as such. Instead the vocal persona of the song is an aspect of the actual singer, expressing himself or herself as a member of a specific community taking part in a ritual or assisting at a social event.[6] In such songs, we are not interested in the words for their meaning, but in their "availability as ritual symbols."[7] Cone includes hymns in this category, and "Happy Birthday" is another classic example.

I propose a different classification of songs than Cone's, one that recognizes three kinds of songs. My taxonomy is based on a song's function and the significance it may hold in cultural contexts, rather than on its genre, musical style, or lyrical content. Organizing songs in the way I suggest allows us to look for similarities of propositional content and musical style among a wide variety of songs that may not readily suggest commonalities. I would also argue that function and cultural role are under-appreciated factors in philosophical thinking about music, and so considering them at the outset may be helpful.

First, while any song can be performed in front of an audience, some songs are "works for performance," specifically intended to be performed, often in a formal setting.[8] These include art songs, songs in opera and music drama, jazz standards, and the songs recorded by professional singers for a mass media audience.

Second are songs intended for "participation-performance" or communal singing. The "audience" and the performers are one in this case. Such songs include national anthems, hymns, camp-fire songs, and many folk songs. Even when only one person performs such a song, he or she does so less *for* an audience than on behalf of an audience.[9]

Finally, some songs are best understood as "purpose-driven" because they serve specific practical or cultural functions. Examples include lullabies, mnemonic songs, work songs, and laments. While purpose-driven songs may be becoming less common as shared physical labor becomes less prevalent in the developed world (with people toiling at desks rather than in fields), they are still important in the education of children.

With this taxonomy in mind, we can begin to consider what singers are doing when they sing.

Singers as Performers (Some First Steps)

Any act of singing – with friends at the pub, to a sleepy child, or in the course of a ritual – may be attended to *as if* it were a performance, but not every act of singing counts as a performance. I take "performance" to be an evaluative concept. A performance, even a bad performance, must fulfill some criteria. Here, as elsewhere in the book, I draw on Stan Godlovitch's account of musical performance. For him, playing (or singing) is not the same as performing (a song). Performing is a species of playing; other types of playing (that are also not performing) are sight-reading, rehearsing, practicing, jamming, and so on.[10] Two of Godlovitch's conditions for performance are most crucial for my purposes. First, a performance is presented before a third party and intended to be received by a third party who listens with active concentrated attention. No audience (or an inattentive audience) means that the event was not a performance. Second, performances are the result of musical agency and skilled activity; they are the outcome of "appropriately creditworthy physical skill."[11] So an amateur who luckily happens to sing a note-perfect rendition of a song has not performed it if she has not developed the skills to support her musical activity.

Why accept Godlovitch's account (aside from its many virtues that I cannot recount here)? As an amateur musician, the distinction between performing and other modes of playing makes a great deal of sense to me. Performance is special; there are works I can play (barely) that I don't feel ready to perform. However, I realize that not everyone will share my intuitions and that appeals to intuition or to common usage are a risky philosophical move. Godlovitch's "skills" requirement allows us to see the difference between singing a song (whether in front of an audience or not) and performing it. Someone who has never taken steps to develop vocal skills and who gets up at an "open mike" night or in a karaoke bar and sings a song has not performed it, regardless of how pleasant the effect. As Godlovitch says, "Causing the sound one intends to cause requires control over one's actions and the instruments of action," and control requires skill.[12] The difference between what the "open mike" singer has done and what a trained singer might do are differences of kind, not degree. I should add that there are many ways to develop vocal skills and I don't mean to limit the discussion to classical singers or those who have attended conservatory, etc. Singing in a choir is a way to develop vocal skills, and some prominent jazz singers developed primarily through their work with instrumentalists. ("I stole everything I ever heard, but mostly I stole from the horns," said Ella Fitzgerald.)[13]

Let's begin with an ideal or exemplary case: professional or semi-professional (that is, appropriately skilled, however these skills have been developed) solo singers who sing works intended for performance, in front of an audience, with or without musical accompaniment. I should mention that not every vocal performance is a rendition of a work for performance or even of a song, and in this I depart somewhat from Godlovitch. Singers may also improvise new lyrics for an existing song, and singers in the jazz tradition may compose or improvise lyrics for an instrumental melodic line ("vocalese") or improvise nonsense syllables ("scat singing") in the course of a song performance.

I began this chapter by stressing that singing is not merely a physical activity but also one imbued with social and cultural expectations. The question, "What do singers do?" might be answered by, "They communicate to an audience." Singing can be understood as a form of verbal communication. While this conception of singing is far from adequate, it will work as a starting place. But *what* do singers communicate when they sing? We must resist the obvious answer that a singer communicates a song's lyrics. For reasons that will take me a couple of chapters fully to spell out, singing cannot be reduced to verbal communication or to communication of a text.

The precise (or nearly precise) communication of song lyrics is expected less often than one might think. As songs are a form of oral communication they are subject to the burdens and limitations of oral communication. We saw in Chapter 1 that song texts tend to be redundant and to trade in familiar simplifications. The fact that singers in a number of traditions (those with "thin" texts) have the latitude to alter lyrics would seem to indicate that conveying the nuances of a particular text in a fixed order is not necessary, at least not in those traditions. Listeners notoriously mishear and misunderstand lyrics. It is very likely that some of the differences in folk song texts through the years can be explained, not only by deliberate alteration on the part of performers, but by singers mishearing and misremembering lyrics. There are entire websites and a small academic literature devoted to such misapprehensions in popular music.[14] (My own favorite example is from an acquaintance who thought that the Police song "Canary in a Coal Mine" was about "Larry, in a coma.")

We can see that singers communicate more than a text when we compare singing performances to other types of public verbal communication. To begin with a distant comparison, singing a song is not much like giving a speech or reading a paper at an academic gathering. In reading an academic paper, the text is the primary element to be communicated. If Smith is

stranded by a snowstorm and cannot get to her session in time, her coll-
eague Jones can read the paper without too much loss, provided Jones is
a competent reader. If Smith is a notorious mumbler or otherwise difficult to
understand, we may be relieved that Jones will read the paper instead. Nor
is most public singing quite like poetry recitations or public literary readings. In literary readings, as at academic conferences, the communication of
the text is crucial. This is not to deny that poets and novelists convey other
things beside their texts and that we see them for other reasons than to hear
a text. We may watch an author present his work in the hope of gaining
insight into it, or in order to make the name on the cover of the book into a
real human being, or even in pursuit of the author's autograph. Still, the
communication of a particular text is of primary importance. Poetry texts
would seem to be ontologically thicker than many song texts.

Since songs are music and singing can be a form of musical performance,
it seems plausible to compare singing with other kinds of musical performances. Philosophers have tended to assume that instrumental music provides the greatest philosophical challenges, and few have focused on the
intricacies and complications of singing as opposed to other kinds of musical
performances. They have tended to underestimate the philosophical importance and complexity of songs and singing. To be fair, the presence of language and meaning in a song adds a further dimension that might needlessly
complicate a general account of a musical performance. Singers are musicians, but what they do is different than what instrumentalists do. Because
singers make music with their bodies, instead of or in addition to musical
instruments, vocal performances have an element of subjectivity beyond that
of solely instrumental performances. A personal "voice" is both an overused
metaphor for individual style and a literal matter of copyright law in many
countries. (I'll have more to say about this in the next chapter, when we
consider singers and audiences.)

One of the few thinkers to consider singing performance in its own right
was Adam Smith (1723–90), better known for his writings on economics.
Smith's insightful analysis of singing performance deserves to be more widely
considered. In keeping with the attitudes to music then current in Britain,
Smith understood music as a form of artistic representation, such that individual musical works may represent the sentiments of a particular person in a
particular situation. In the case of a vocal performance, an additional layer of
representation, beyond that of the music, is possible. The singer can, "by his
countenance, by his attitudes, by his gestures, and by his motions," convey the
sentiments of the person whose situation is depicted in the song.[15] The singer's acting enhances the performance and is indeed necessary for a good performance. As Smith writes, "there is no comparison between the effect of what
is sung coldly from a music-book at the end of a harpsichord, and of what is
not only sung, but acted with proper freedom, animation, and boldness."[16]

The idea that some singing may be like acting seems promising. Like an
actor, a singer may inhabit a role. This seems obviously true of singers in

opera and other forms of musical drama, and also true of at least some other kinds of songs. A successful performance of a song should make us believe (or make-believe) that the singer actually is experiencing the emotions and living through the experiences conveyed in the song. A good performance can make us believe that the singer is falling in love ("This Could Be the Start of Something Big"), or feeling sad at the end of an affair ("Smoke Gets in Your Eyes"), or contrite and rueful ("You Were Always on My Mind"). Our rational selves know (or should know) that the singer may be none of these things. Indeed, a performer who sang these three songs in succession simply could not go through such a sequence of emotional ups and downs and still complete the songs.

Clearly there are elements of acting in singing, even in singing that is not a part of a musical drama. Singers may express emotions they do not actually feel, and they may be compelled, in singing a song, to adopt the perspective of narrators whose personality and values do not reflect their own. Only the most naïve listeners fail to acknowledge some elements of pretense in singing performance. Yet there are limits to the comparison between acting and singing, and not just because singing is a form of musical performance and acting, in itself, is not (although it may be combined with musical performance). Emotion and narrative perspective can be successfully feigned and accepted by audiences; there will be limits to audience acceptance of the performance of gender, age, and race. Unlike actors, singers in recital can make limited use of make-up and costume, to say nothing of resources like body doubles and computer generated imagery to which film actors have access.[17] While we accept for the most part that actors play at being someone else, we expect singers, at some level, to be "themselves."

Like Smith, Cone (whose taxonomy of songs I considered earlier in this chapter) also stresses the elements of acting and pretense within singing. He approaches these issues through an intriguing question about vocal performance and song meaning. In listening to, say, a performance of Schubert's setting of a poem by Goethe, whose voice do we hear? He suggests four different answers. We hear (1) the actual physical voice of the singer in question; (2) the protagonist of the song; (3) the poet (Goethe) whose words and images characterize the protagonist and the dramatic situation; (4) and in the song's musical accompaniment we hear the voice of the composer (Schubert). Yet the composer is not simply one voice among the four. Rather, the voice of the composer constitutes the "complete musical persona," and the vocal persona – the protagonist of the song – is properly understood as a character quoted by the complete persona. The complete musical persona of a song is not to be strictly identified with the composer but is "a projection of [the composer's] musical intelligence, constituting the mind, so to speak, of the composition in question."[18]

This analysis of song meaning leads Cone to a specific understanding of song performance, one that emphasizes the importance of dramatic impersonation. In Cone's example, when Marian Anderson sings "Swing Low,

Sweet Chariot," she recreates, as a dramatic persona, the slave who originally sang the song as an authentic appeal. An ideal or "faithful" performance is one in which the physical presence and vitality of the singer turns the persona of the musical text into an immediate living being. By contrast, in an illegitimate interpretation, it is the singer (rather than the vocal persona) who is seen as embodying and "composing" the song as he or she sings. The singer fails to let us hear the persona – and hence the composer's voice behind the persona – speak for itself.

What Counts as a *Successful* Singing Performance?

I introduced the work of Smith and Cone in order to explore the similarities between singer and acting, all the while in pursuit of an answer to the question, "What do singers do?" But both Smith and Cone quickly moved from claims about performances to claims about "ideal" and "faithful" performance (for Cone) and an "enhanced" or "good" performance (Smith). This is a time-honored philosophical move: in trying to understand "X" reflect upon what an excellent or exemplary "X" might be like. Considering an ideal "X" might help us understand "X"s in general. So one way to try to get more clear on what singing is, is to think of the characteristics of an excellent or successful singing performance. I would like to continue this line of inquiry before getting back to the similarities between singing and acting.

Now, I may have just lost some readers. I can almost hear my critics: "Just because *you* think someone is a good singer doesn't mean that the rest of us have to agree. Everyone has a right to their own opinion. It's all relative, anyway. I find your attitude here *judgmental*. Isn't it even *oppressive* to say that some people are better singers than others? A post-modern perspective allows for a multiplicity of ways of being and vocalizing ... "

Let me make my commitments explicit and at least begin my defense of them: some people are better singers than others. We may not be able fully to spell out what it is for one person to be a "better" singer than another. There is likely to be controversy over who the "better" singers are. People may legitimately have different opinions about whom the better singers are, and they may even have different opinions about what counts as good singing. But the right to hold an opinion is not the same as the right to have one's opinion acknowledged as correct. We can respectfully disagree with others yet accept their right to hold their opinion.

Sometimes we appreciate the beauty of a singer's tone, which is largely a product of their physiology. Sometimes we appreciate how a singer uses the voice – the way he or she shapes phrases, expresses emotion, and draws our attention to certain words. A person may have a beautiful-sounding voice (thanks to their physiology) but be unable (whether through lack of interest or lack of vocal training) to use the voice in a musically effective way. A vocalist may be a good singer (or even a great singer) in the second sense, without having an exceptional voice. Take Bob Dylan, for example. Even the people who praise him as a singer acknowledge that he does not have a beautiful voice. Those who appreciate him do so for different reasons: his expressiveness and the quality of sincerity in his voice. In his essay on Dylan for *Rolling Stone*'s "100 Greatest Singers" feature, Bono recounts that Sam Cooke, in explaining Dylan's appeal to another performer said, "From now on, it's not going to be about how pretty the voice is. It's going to be about believing that the voice is telling the truth."[19]

To be sure, there is disagreement over the relative quality of singers and different people may prefer different kinds of music and different vocal styles. (I myself was a little surprised to see Dylan as high as no. 7 on the *Rolling Stone* list.) Yet these differences do not imply that there is no fact of the matter about who is a good singer and no way to decide such questions. And while we find controversy in the arts we also find pockets of broad agreement and consensus. Maria Callas, Ella Fitzgerald, Frank Sinatra, and Dietrich Fischer-Dieskau are considered to be among the greatest vocalists of the twentieth century. It would be perverse to argue that they were not so considered, and there would be nothing inconsistent with acknowledging the greatness of Callas or Fitzgerald even if you don't like to listen to opera or jazz.

At the same time, it is only fair and reasonable for me to acknowledge the element of truth in the relativist's critique. What counts as being a "good" singer will indeed be relative to different audiences. Different audiences (even different individual listeners) will have different expectations of singers. The excellence of Sinatra is not the excellence of Fischer-Dieskau. Their work belongs to different musical genres (jazz and popular singing as opposed to art singing) and fulfills different (to some degree) expectations. Even within the same tradition there are different ways of being a good singer – Nina Simone and Jo Stafford were both exemplary female jazz vocalists, yet they are appreciated for different reasons.

So with this skepticism towards relativism, combined with a nod to the element of truth it holds, what can we now say about *successful* or *exemplary* song performance?

In the previous chapter I argued that a good song is one that provides listeners with a good experience. My views on good singing performance follow the same line. A good singing performance is one that provides listeners with a good or rich experience. What this means for a specific song is likely to depend on the textual and musical qualities of the song itself, the performance tradition in which it is embedded, and the audience expectations it meets or fails to meet. Listeners of all musical traditions, despite their differing expectations, take pleasure in good performances. So while being a great rock singer is different in many ways from being a great jazz singer, there will be some overlap in what good singers do and in audience responses in either case.

Listeners take pleasure, but to do this they must be convinced by the singer and by the singer performing that particular song. What do I mean?

At a minimal level, to be convinced by a performance is to be engaged by it. A listener who stops listening (for whatever reason) cannot be convinced, and one cannot take pleasure in a musical performance one has not heard. But this is just the first step or initial condition. One can be engaged by a performance because it is so bad or so strange. Listeners stop being convinced when there is some kind of incongruity within a performance to distract their attention from that performance.

Many kinds of incongruities can distract us from attending to a musical performance. These include musical errors such as incorrect pitches or errors in rhythm in those musical genres where a high degree of accuracy is expected. Another example might be a disjunction between the sentiments expressed in a song and by the singer's performance, as in a loud, boisterous performance of a soulful, melancholy song. The notion of conviction I have in mind is not completely rational – songs are not arguments, after all. A successful performance of a song might move an audience in various ways, from delight to sadness to chagrin. Such emotional responses (when befitting the song in question) count as evidence of an audience's having been engaged and convinced.

How important is the communication of text to an audience's being "convinced"? Depending on musical genre and audience expectations, that a singer conveys the precise words of a text may be more or less important. If you do not expect to be able to understand the lyrics, then a failure to hear them will not be an incongruity that distracts from the performance. The fact that a number of hit recordings of rock and pop music document performances in which the lyrics cannot be made out would seem to indicate that at least some audiences do not need to hear a song's words in order to take pleasure in its performance. So there must be more to successful communication of a song than successful communication of the song's lyrics. It is easy to imagine examples where, for the audience to be convinced, other factors are equally important, if not more important, than the exact communication of a text. Think of a performance of the traditional American song "In the Pines" (also known as "Where Did You Sleep Last Night?") in which the lyrics were perfectly comprehensible but none of the song's strong emotion was conveyed. I do not think it would hold audiences' attention, or that we would consider it to be a successful performance.

With some songs (like "In the Pines"), the communication of a dominant emotional mood or a specific rhythmic feel are just as important as the communication of the lyrics. Many blues songs are in this category. Despite the differences implied by genre and tradition, it is safe to say that the successful communication of a text is not always necessary for a successful singing performance, and it is never sufficient. Even in genres where it is the expectation that lyrics are understandable, such as opera and art song, there is more going on. Joan Sutherland, the Australian soprano, was sometimes criticized for poor diction because she changed some of her vowel sounds ever so slightly. Yet this shortcoming did not bar her from being considered

one of the greatest opera singers of the twentieth century. Just as communication of a text is not necessarily required for singing, it is not necessarily
required for successful singing. Singers communicate more than a text; so do
successful singers. Again, song is music and text is not.

I have already discussed some of the incongruities that might hinder successful communication of a song and leave an audience unconvinced.
Obviously, a poor performance might leave an audience unconvinced and
unable to take pleasure in a song. Arguably, performance choices that are at
odds with what the song conveys in a standard or typical performance might
be unconvincing. Examples might include a syntactically precise but emotionally flat rendition of a blues song or of a song whose lyrics convey loss
and heartbreak. However, not every "eccentric" performance choice leads to
failure of audience conviction – a good singer can make seemingly inappropriate decisions with little resulting loss of aesthetic interest. For example, Nina Simone's up-tempo, almost "chatty" rendition of "Mood Indigo"
strikes me as aesthetically defensible, as does Barbra Streisand's dirge-like
rendition of "Happy Days Are Here Again." Simone and Streisand succeed
in highlighting aspects of these songs that are obscured in more standard
renditions. There can be exhilaration just behind the bluest moods – a silver
lining can conceal a cloud. When singing "against" a song in this way is
successful, I suspect it is because the aesthetic experience offered is sufficiently rich to be pleasurable for audiences. Not every questionable or
"against the grain" performance choice will be aesthetically successful. Some
may be interesting enough to provoke a response of "isn't that clever" or
"how odd." While there are elements of pleasure in such reactions, these
responses are not reliable or enduring enough to constitute sustained aesthetic
payoff.

To sum up: I have offered only a partial answer to the question, "What
do singers do?" and I have begun to consider the similarities between singing
and acting. Singers communicate to an audience, and, for those singers who
are performers, successful singing means communicating in such a way that
audiences are convinced enough to be engaged. If audiences are not engaged,
they will not be able to take pleasure in a performance, and I have argued
that a good or successful performance is one that offers audiences a rich
experience. So far I have limited the discussion to singers singing works
intended for performance. Performances require audiences and, to get a
deeper understanding of singing, we will need to discuss audiences.

"Yesterday"

The words and music of "Yesterday" were written by Paul McCartney and
he is the only band member featured on the 1965 recording credited to "The
Beatles." He sings and plays acoustic guitar, accompanied by a string quartet. According to an article in the British newspaper *The Independent*,
"Yesterday" is the second most covered song ever[20] and Wikipedia claims

that there have been over 2,200 cover versions.[21] (The most covered song is "Eleanor Rigby," also by the Beatles.) "Yesterday" has been recorded by other pop artists, as well as by jazz, country, and operatic singers. What can we learn about successful song performance by considering some of the many versions?

Because "Yesterday" has been covered so many times and by artists in so many different musical traditions, I felt sure that I would find a variety of approaches and many contrasting examples to discuss. To my surprise, with very few exceptions, singers have approached this song in similar ways. Few have strayed beyond the vocal template set by McCartney in his original recording: slow, regular rhythm in common (4/4) time, the lyrics sung mainly on the beat, with an overall feeling of nostalgia and regret.[22] Every word is audible. Marianne Faithful, who also recorded the song in 1965, replaced the string quartet with what sounds like an angelic choir, but otherwise makes no significant changes.[23] The Supremes (1966) are tasteful and restrained, almost too much so.[24] Michael Bolton (1992) sounds overwrought.[25] The a cappella version by Boyz II Men (1994) is notable for the gorgeous harmonies and the addition of a new lyric at the end of the song ("Yesterday was so far away/ And I know I can't turn back cause yesterday is gone").[26] Turning from pop to country, Ray Price (1968),[27] Tammy Wynette (also 1968),[28] and Willie Nelson on a live album (1966),[29] and in the studio with Merle Haggard (1987)[30] are all similarly deferential. They sing slowly and clearly enough that the words can be understood and make few changes to the song's text. It is almost a relief to come across a film of Elvis Presley in rehearsal (1970)[31] mixing up the words and gently mocking the song by looking around for the "shadow hanging over me." Yet his professionalism comes through long enough that he manages to sound sincere and heartfelt in the places where it counts.

In describing the sources of vocal technique in rock singing, Richard Middleton writes that twentieth century popular singing has been subject to pressure by a rising "aesthetic of sincerity."[32] I think this is a wonderful phrase. Sincerity – what we usually think of as the genuine or "true" expression of thought or feeling – is seen as a mode of performance. Rather than reflecting the inner state or emotion of a singer, it is instead (or in addition) a way of adhering to audience expectations. And I don't think that the demand for an aesthetic of sincerity is limited to popular music, although among listeners there may be more or less willingness to accept singers as interpreters in their own right. Less sophisticated listeners may have increased difficulty recognizing the possible distance between singers and their material. To my ear, the opera singers who have recorded "Yesterday" sound just as respectful, sincere, and genuine as the pop and country artists I have mentioned. American soprano Cathy Berberian (1967) adds a harpsichord to the string quartet and sings in an open and straightforward way.[33] (Well, this is how I hear her; a musical friend I discussed this with hears her performance as an ironic commentary on popular music.)

Berberian and tenor Placido Domingo (who recorded "Yesterday" in 1981)[34] are of course both operatically trained and their voices sound significantly different from the other singers I've been discussing. Yet they too make sure that we can hear every word, they sing on the beat, and convey emotions of sadness and regret (more restrained in Berberian's case than Domingo's).

One of the points I have been stressing is that while singing is a physical activity, it is subject to a variety of social and cultural expectations. Singers who perform for audiences must also negotiate the expectations of their audience, which may vary according to musical genre and other factors. While the singers I have mentioned do not stray far from the prototype set by McCartney, each sings the song in a way that is respectful of their established audience. The country singers sound recognizably like country singers and the arrangements they use adhere to country music conventions. The Supremes sound like the Supremes. And while Berberian and Domingo still sound like opera singers, each signals to their fans to expect something a little out of the ordinary: Berberian by calling her album *Beatles Arias* and Domingo by the words "with John Denver" on his album cover. Although Denver is featured on only two of the ten tracks, presumably the mention of the popular country/adult-contemporary star alerted listeners that the music within would not be the standard operatic repertoire.

I did not hear "Yesterday" sung in a significantly different way until I explored some of the R&B artists who covered it. Stax recording artist Carla Thomas ("The Queen of Memphis Soul") makes the song her own in a live recording from 1967.[35] She shifts it from pop to soul by playing with the vocal line rhythm, stretching out some of the lyrics, repeating others, and using gospel-music flavored melisma. My favorite, of all the versions I listened to, was the one by Marvin Gaye (1970).[36] He all but re-writes the song, using a different musical arrangement, adding syncopation, slipping into his falsetto range in the bridge, and placing the song firmly in the soul/R&B genre.

I have argued that in order for listeners to take pleasure in a singer's performance, they must first be convinced to engage with it. A listener accustomed to pop voices might not be able to appreciate an operatically trained voice and the renditions of "Yesterday" by Berberian or Domingo might sound incongruous. Fans of opera and art music might find it similarly incongruous to hear classically trained voices singing pop. And while historians of popular music may recognize that the music of the Beatles shares some common influences with country music, fans of the two genres might not be prepared to acknowledge their similarities. Perhaps that is why Willie Nelson, before singing "Yesterday," jokes with the audience that he will do a song recorded by "a pretty fair little country group" and then adds that "seriously" he appreciates the song very much as a songwriter. He frames "Yesterday" so that his singing of it will be acceptable to his audience of country music fans.

Of all of the artists I listened to, the only performance that failed to convince me was by Michael Bolton. To my taste, there was just too much incongruity between the simplicity and restraint of the tune and the words and his over-wrought treatment of them. In the end, he sounded cheesy – particularly from about halfway through the song. And while Thomas and Gaye both express strong emotion, I do not hear them as over-doing it. I suspect that taking the song out of pop and into soul makes their level of expressivity more acceptable. Bolton, who stays in pop or easy-listening, ends up stretching pop conventions a little too far.

The thoughts and sentiments expressed by "Yesterday" – nostalgia for the past tinged with regret – are general enough they will resonate with almost anyone. I think that must be part of the song's appeal. It also means that it is a song that is appropriate for nearly all singers, without regard for culture, race, physical appearance, or musical genre. (Although it might be strange to hear a very young singer perform "Yesterday.") But not all songs are appropriate for all singers, and some singers will be unable to convince an audience if they choose to perform certain songs. In the next chapter, we explore these complications.

Notes

1 From his interview with Klaus R. Scherer in "The Singer's Paradox: On Authenticity in Emotional Expression on the Opera Stage," in Tom Cochrane, Bernardo Fantini & Klaus R. Scherer (eds), *The Emotional Power of Music* (Oxford: Oxford University Press, 2013), 64.
2 George List, "The Boundaries of Speech and Song," *Ethnomusicology* 7 (1963), 4–13.
3 As of writing I have not found this article.
4 Edward Cone, *The Composer's Voice* (Berkeley: University of California Press, 1974), 58.
5 Cone, *The Composer's Voice*, 59.
6 Cone, *The Composer's Voice*, 49–52.
7 Cone, *The Composer's Voice*, 50.
8 See Paul Thom, *For an Audience: A Philosophy of the Performing Arts* (Philadelphia: Temple University Press, 1993), Chapter 1; and Stephen Davies, *Musical Works and Performances: A Philosophical Exploration* (Oxford: Clarendon Press, 2001), 20–25.
9 My thinking on this is indebted to Victor Zuckerkandl, *Man the Musician* (Princeton: Princeton University Press, 1973), 27.
10 Stan Godlovitch, *Musical Performance: A Philosophical Study* (London: Routledge, 1998), 12–13.
11 Godlovitch, *Musical Performance*, 49.
12 Godlovitch, *Musical Performance*, 18.
13 www.ellafitzgerald.com/about/quote.html (accessed December 11, 2014).
14 Kevin J.H. Dettmar, "There Must Be Some Misunderstanding: Unintelligible Rock Lyrics Can Teach Us What We Think," *The Chronicle of Higher Education* March 17, 2014. https://chronicle.com/article/There-Must-Be-Some/145273/ (accessed March 22, 2014).
15 Adam Smith, "Of the Nature of that Imitation Which Takes Place in What Are Called the Imitative Arts," in W.P.D. Wightman and J.C. Bryce (eds), *Essays on Philosophical Subjects*, (Indianapolis: Liberty Fund, 1982 [1795]), 194.
16 Smith, "Of the Nature of that Imitation," 194.

17 The situation is different for opera singers and singers in dramatic productions. I consider them in Chapter 8.

18 Cone, *The Composer's Voice*, 57.

19 See   www.rollingstone.com/music/lists/100-greatest-singers-of-all-time-19691231/bob-dylan-20101202#ixzz2yIlDSsjg (accessed April 7, 2014).

20 www.independent.co.uk/arts-entertainment/music/features/the-10-most-covered-songs-1052165.html (accessed April 7, 2014).

21 http://en.wikipedia.org/wiki/Yesterday (accessed April 7, 2014).

22 http://youtu.be/2WQAl5nJWHs (accessed December 9, 2014).

23 http://youtu.be/gORyrU1xQpg (accessed December 9, 2014).

24 http://youtu.be/6m700Z2ewu8 (accessed December 9, 2014).

25 http://youtu.be/pl-M0_yEyLA (accessed December 9, 2014).

26 http://youtu.be/C6J50Pjd9jA (accessed December 9, 2014).

27 http://youtu.be/XgDqvf29sFE (accessed December 9, 2014).

28 http://youtu.be/xSVtm_gwvBY (accessed December 9, 2014).

29 http://youtu.be/G_hT_5iScis (accessed December 9, 2014).

30 http://youtu.be/W64pgAcKbYA (accessed December 9, 2014).

31 http://youtu.be/P7TwXr79_qQ (accessed December 9, 2014).

32 Richard Middleton, "Rock Singing," in John Potter (ed.), *The Cambridge Companion to Singing* (Cambridge: Cambridge University Press, 2000), 32.

33 http://youtu.be/GvuxldwxW8k (accessed December 9, 2014).

34 http://youtu.be/HRRP9TwON3I (accessed December 9, 2014).

35 http://youtu.be/pEGYPWuWuoE (accessed December 9, 2014).

36 http://youtu.be/_VSlNyGpvDQ (accessed December 9, 2014).

4   Singers and Audiences

Would you ask a writer if his book is real or fiction? It's just a song.

(P. Diddy – Sean Combs)

Listeners sometimes make assumptions about singers' inner lives based on the songs they sing. In 1987, when Bruce Springsteen released the album *Tunnel of Love* with its songs of disillusion and estrangement, many fans wondered whether his recent marriage to Julianne Phillips was in trouble. A music journalist asked rapper P. Diddy (Sean Combs) if his hit song "I Need a Girl (Part 1)" expressed his feelings about the aftermath of his relationship with Jennifer Lopez, giving voice to the curiosity many at the time felt.[1] Why do listeners look for, and indeed often assume, connections between singers' repertoire and their actual lives? Do we expect emotional "authenticity" from singers, such that their selection of repertoire and actions in performance must reflect their true inner states?

Springsteen and Combs write their own material and so may be particularly burdened with such expectations. Yet similar expectations about the relationship between performers and songs seem to operate even for singers who do not write their own material. The African-American singer and actor Paul Robeson (1898–1976) was a supporter of the Civil Rights Movement and a staunch advocate for social justice, even to the point of joining the Communist Party at a time when doing so invited personal and financial hardship. Would we not be disappointed if we learned that when he sang "Go Down Moses" (with the repeated line, "Let my people go") he regarded the spiritual as just a song, with scant relevance to his own life or to the lives of African-Americans more generally?

Some readers might raise the objection that only unsophisticated listeners make connections between a singer's life and the songs that he or she sings. But I think that such assumptions, while perhaps most frequently made by fans of popular music, are made by listeners across many different genres. In 2009 the Italian opera singer Cecilia Bartoli released an album of music originally written for castrati – adult male sopranos who were castrated before puberty so that their voices would not develop normally. She said that the pyrotechnic pieces were not as hard to sing as the "beautiful sad" arias, because she found these almost unbearably moving: "I know they were singing those arias out of their own sorrow."[2]

In this chapter I confront a cluster of questions concerning the relationship between audiences and singers. What relationship do listeners assume between the performer and whatever is communicated by a song, and why do they assume this relationship? What expectations do audiences impose on singers, and how do these expectations shape vocal performance? I think it is clear that we do make certain assumptions about the relationship between singers and songs. I hinted at this in the previous chapter, when I introduced the notion of listeners needing to be "convinced" by the song and the singer before they could take pleasure in a performance. One aspect of this "conviction" is that our expectations regarding which songs are appropriate for which singers should not be violated. I mentioned earlier that "Yesterday" is a song that is appropriate for almost any singer (except perhaps a very young person) and that this was one of the reasons why it has been so widely covered. Before I can say more about listeners' expectations, I need to step back and consider musical performance more generally.

Music Performance

I introduced Stan Godlovitch's philosophical account of musical performance in the previous chapter as the most elaborated and cogent that I know. His analysis is particularly valuable in pointing out some aesthetically significant and rewarding aspects of performance that are all too often overlooked. According to Godlovitch, performances are large, complex, integrated events which draw together sounds, agents, works, and listeners.[3] With further analysis of each of these components, performance emerges as "a complex activity which co-ordinates and focuses actions, skills, traditions, and works in order to define and create musical experience for the receptive listener."[4] Godlovitch (and I follow him in this) accords more weight to the performer–listener axis than to the composer–performer relationship. While performances can fail by misrepresenting works, performers do not have unconditional obligations to composers. However, performers do indeed have certain categorical obligations to listeners, and performances can also fail by disaffecting listeners.[5]

Turning to the role of human intentional agency in performance, Godlovitch devises and reflects on a clever thought experiment. Could a very sophisticated computer simulator be said to give a performance? His answer is no. In coming to this answer Godlovitch identifies and illuminates some of the features audiences find important in performance. To summarize his conclusions: we expect that musical performances are by persons, and to exclude the performer's physical presence and behaviour from the aesthetic experience would seem an "unintelligible deprivation."[6] As Godlovitch writes, "We are drawn to personal details, and these seamlessly intertwine with our aesthetic expectations; for example, the riotous life of the performer, his cranky, immature conduct at august gatherings, his wayward attitude to his listeners, his crippling depressions, his bitter envy of his colleagues, his rapt intensity on stage, his savage career ambitions, and the like."[7] Finally, "artist and artwork, performance and performer are quite as inseparable as people are from their histories, external and internal."[8]

Godlovitch emphasizes instrumental performance because the presence of language and meaning in song needlessly complicates the general picture. However, his account, with its stress on the concrete physicality and distinctive personality of the performer, can help us bring out some of the particular difficulties posed by vocal performance. As I have suggested, we make assumptions about the appropriateness or "fit" of the relationship between singers and songs that we do not so readily make regarding instrumentalists and their material. Our expectations regarding which songs are appropriate for which singers go beyond similar expectations for instrumentalists and their repertoires. If these expectations are thwarted or violated, there will be negative consequences for aesthetic experience.

Singers and Personas

The notion of a "public persona" is crucial to my discussion of audience expectations. A singer's public persona is the face, body, and personal history he or she presents to the audience. It includes such factors as gender, race, age, and ethnicity, as well as quirks of personality such as those Godlovitch describes. This information may be conveyed by the singer's appearance, clothing and accessories, repertoire, and the statements and activities reported by the media or circulated among fans. A public persona may transparently reflect elements of a singer's "true" personality; more likely it will be mediated and constructed to some degree. While an instrumentalist's public persona plays a role in our experience of his or her performances in much the way Godlovitch lays out, a singer's public persona plays an even greater part in our experience. In particular, it is critical in shaping our expectations regarding which songs are appropriate for which singers.

"Appropriate" here could be understood in several different ways. I have in mind aesthetic appropriateness as opposed to moral, legal, or practical appropriateness. There may indeed be songs (and some ways of performing songs) that are not morally appropriate for certain singers, and I set aside such complications for another chapter. Aesthetic appropriateness, of course, includes considerations such as whether a song is suitable to the singer's ability and vocal range, but it is not exhausted by such considerations. Similarly, considerations of aesthetic appropriateness go beyond the question of whether a work is drawn from outside the singer's established genre. Such crossovers are often accepted by audiences and can be aesthetically interesting. Examples might include some of the many covers of "Yesterday" we considered in the previous chapter. Country singer Johnny Cash gained a new audience in the last years of his life with recordings of material outside the country genre, including U2's "One," Nick Cave's "The Mercy Seat," and Trent Reznor's "Hurt." Pop/adult-contemporary singer Tom Jones' cover of Prince's electro-funk "Kiss" was a hit and Run DMC's rap over Aerosmith's hard rock "Walk This Way" was one of the biggest hits of the 1980s. So while adherence to a specific type of repertoire might be important for some audiences, it would seem that listeners are mostly willing to be tolerant of their favorite artists making unexpected song choices.

A vocal performance can *fail* to be aesthetically appropriate when the public persona of the singer inhibits the successful communication of whatever is crucial in the song. If there is too great an incongruity between the singer's public persona and the song, audiences may fail to be convinced. I said earlier that listeners' acceptance of *this* particular singer as appropriate for *this* song and vice versa is among the necessary conditions of their taking routine or standard pleasure in the performance of a song. This brings us to considerations of which songs are appropriate for which singers. Some songs are aesthetically appropriate for almost any performer. "Happy Birthday" comes to mind, as do the bulk of standards. But not all songs are appropriate for all singers. Each aspect of a singer's persona can influence which songs an audience would find convincing, were she to decide to perform them. Let's take a closer look at each of these factors in turn.

Some songs are inappropriate for performers above or below certain ages. An incongruity is likely to arise if a young performer sings of weary worldliness ("It Was a Very Good Year," "Thanks for the Memories," "Hum Drum Blues") or if an obviously jaded older performer sings a "youthful" song ("My Heart Belongs to Daddy," "I Feel Pretty," "A Tisket, A Tasket"). A performer's gender is another obvious factor that can affect which songs are aesthetically appropriate. Theodore Gracyk has argued that the authorship of a song attaches to the gendered body of the singer, regardless of our knowledge of actual authorship.[9] (Gracyk is primarily interested in rock music, but the point would seem to hold for a wider range of music.) For example, even if we know that Otis Redding wrote "Respect" and have heard his recording, when we hear Aretha Franklin sing it, it becomes difficult not to think of it as a woman's demand for respect from a man. Gracyk's claim strikes me as largely correct. "(You Make Me Feel Like) A Natural Woman" was co-written by one woman and two men (Carole King, Gerry Goffin, and Jerry Wexler), but I do not know of any male vocalists who could sing it, lyrics unchanged, and hope to convince an audience.

Yet considerations of gender may not be as limiting as we might think at first. "The Girl from Ipanema" has been successfully recorded by both men and women, despite the narrative perspective being male. Nina Simone's rendition of Nat Adderly and Oscar Brown Jr.'s "Work Song" describing life on a chain gang is (to this listener, anyway) no less credible for being sung by a woman, despite the historical fact that there were few women on chain gangs. "Mining for Gold" by the Cowboy Junkies begins with the words, "We are miners, hard rock miners." The performance by Margo Timmins, the female lead vocalist, convinces me – it is only after the song finishes that I am reminded that mining is a notoriously male-dominated profession. I suspect that a performer's gender is salient only in combination with other factors such as race and ethnicity, projected personality, and age. I do not think that just any female vocalist could sing "Work Song" or "Mining for Gold" and convince an audience. Imagine Britney Spears, Jennifer Lopez, or Whitney Houston singing these songs. Simone is able to make us believe in "Work Song," partly because of *who she is* as a performer, not only because of her musical skill and performance choices, although these are certainly factors.

A vocalist's personality is another factor that influences what kinds of songs an audience will accept from her. By "personality" I have in mind only those aspects of character on public display, and some singers will present to the public a "thicker" or more vivid personality than others. I have never met Madonna and know nothing of what she may be "really" like. Elements of her public persona, however, are fairly well established: she presents herself as brash, sexy, driven, difficult, and blunt speaking. I suspect that these elements of Madonna's public persona would make it difficult to accept her rendition of certain types of songs. For example, her public persona would be at odds with the sorrowful monologues ("Don't Explain," "Ain't Nobody's Business," etc.) performed so effectively by Billie Holiday and others. Similarly, Frank Sinatra's public persona for part of his career as a swaggering hipster makes it difficult for me to take seriously his rendition of the Gershwin classic, "Someone to Watch over Me." The vulnerability expressed in the song's lyrics seems incongruous with elements of Sinatra's public persona. I can accept Sinatra drinking in a bar after the end of a love-affair – "One for My Baby (And One for the Road)". But I have trouble believing his self-description as "a little lamb lost in the wood" ("Someone to Watch over Me"). Whether or not Sinatra may have experienced such moments of vulnerability is beside the point; his public persona (at least by the middle-to-late period of his career when I saw him perform the song on TV) seemed at odds with them.

No doubt there is a dialectic in effect here: the kinds of songs a singer typically performs also work to influence audience perception of her personality. An article about music promoter Jason Flom and his struggles in marketing singer Cindy Almouzni (for a time know as "Cherie") illustrates this point nicely. Songwriters were having difficulty creating the right up-tempo number for her, since most dance songs are about sex. Flom explained, "Cherie doesn't sing about sex. She sings about love. So we need a dance song about love. [A recent hit with sexually explicit lyrics] is not the right song for Cherie."[10] An appropriate song choice is seen as reflecting the singer's personality, and this in turn is part of the construction of a public persona.

Race and ethnicity are additional factors which make up what I have called the singer's "public persona" and which influence aesthetic appropriateness and hence audience conviction. I can think of a handful of songs in which the lyrics directly refer to the singer's race. The most famous is probably James Brown's "Say it Loud – I'm Black and I'm Proud" (1968). It was the likely inspiration for the Temptations' "Message from a Black Man" (1969) and rapper Styles P's "I'm Black" (2006). Simone is associated with at least two songs that refer to the singer's African-American racial background: "Four Women" (1966), in which each of the four female narrators represents a different aspect of the legacy of slavery, and "To Be Young, Gifted and Black" (1970).

I doubt that white vocalists could sing these songs in such a way so as to convince an audience, and, if any tried, the failure would not be a failure of musical skill (or only of musical skill). There would be too much incongruity between the lyrics ("My skin is black" or "I'm black and I'm proud") and the performer's appearance, and the incongruity would distract from anything else. In this category we might also include songs that are associated with particular groups, although the narrative voice is not explicitly identified as belonging to a particular race or ethnicity. Examples include "Strange Fruit" and "Go Down, Moses" because of their long association with African-American performers, rather than because of any specific textual references. Audiences who have come to expect black vocalists to sing these songs may not be ready to accept them delivered by non-blacks, and vocalists who are not African-American may in turn be reluctant to perform the songs.

Before ending my discussion of public persona and audience expectations, I need to mention one further complication. So far I have written as though "listeners" and "the audience" are homogenous. No doubt some readers have already suspected that the reality is more complicated. To be sure, different audiences (and different individual listeners) will have different expectations of singers. The audience for jazz singing is not the same as that for pop singing; the audience for Nina Simone is not the same as that for Diana Krall (although in both cases there may be some overlap). Among listeners, there may be more or less willingness to accept singers as interpreters in their own right.

Audience expectations can also change over time. The audience for popular music in the 1940s and 1950s seemed to accept (at least some) singers putting on regional accents. Rosemary Clooney had a big hit with "Come-on-a My House" (1951), a song she disliked but was compelled to record. She kept the same ersatz Italian accent for "Mambo Italiano" (1954), which also became a hit. Ella Fitzgerald and Louis Jordan affect Caribbean accents for "Stone Cold Dead in the Market (He Had it Coming)" (1946). Today these performances seem bizarre, if not vaguely cringe-making. Current audiences seem much more sensitive to issues of respect and cultural appropriation. (As singer Katy Perry found out when she was widely derided for performing in a Geisha costume at the 2013 American Music Awards.)

Even if we allow that audience expectations can change with time, if there is too great an incongruity or mismatch between a singer's public persona and what is conveyed in a particular song, audiences will fail to be convinced. They will not accept this song from this singer and so will be inhibited from taking pleasure in the performance. Of the factors that comprise a singer's public persona, race and gender would seem to be most firmly entrenched and difficult to "sing against," although I have argued that personality can influence an audience's perception of gender appropriateness.

A singer might exploit the incongruity between her public persona and a particular song for the sake of humor or other reasons. Singers may have goals in performance other than convincing an audience. I do not deny that there may be aesthetic payoffs in say, Madonna singing the blues or Bruce Springsteen singing "The Man I Love." Yet the distancing effect likely to be produced by such performances would work against the experience of routine or standard pleasure. Certainly, whatever pleasure one might take in (white comedian) Sandra Bernhard's performance of Simone's "Four Women" in *Without You I'm Nothing,* the 1990 film of her off-Broadway show, it is not the same kind of pleasure we would take in the performance of a black female vocalist singing the song.

Personal Beauty and the Public Persona

A friend who teaches in the music department of a major university told me that she can always tell which of her graduate students are singers the moment they walk into class. Not only are they better dressed than the instrumentalists, generally, they are all fairly good-looking. She adds (ruefully, I think), "I guess one doesn't get very far without that."

Keith Richards writes that when he was listening to American music in London in the early 1960s, he didn't know that Chuck Berry was black for two years after he first heard the music, and he didn't know that Jerry Lee Lewis was white "for ages."[11] It is hard to imagine contemporary fans not knowing what a singer they admire looks like. For better or worse, we have ready access to visual representations of the singers we hear. And while we are all told as children not to "judge a book by its cover," we all do this to some degree. There is ample research that being good-looking is advantageous. Better-looking people are better paid than their average counterparts, they are less likely to be convicted of crimes, and, when they are, they usually get lighter sentences.[12]

I suspect that, just as we assume better-looking people to be smarter and nicer, we also assume they will be better singers. Consider some of the tropes invoked by television programs such as *The Voice,* the "Idol" series, and those that proclaim that some particular geographic location has "Got Talent." In one typical scenario the audience is presented with a contestant who is not conventionally good-looking, may speak with a strong regional accent, is badly dressed, perhaps with bad teeth, and whose self-presentation is decidedly unglamorous, not to say dowdy or bumpkin-like. The singer announces his or her chosen song – usually something rather difficult for an amateur to sing well. We see close-ups of the audience rolling their eyes, the "tough" judge looking impatient and the "nice" female judge evidently uncomfortable. Clearly we are all being set up to be amused by the singer's approaching failure.

Instead, the unattractive singer sings beautifully. The audience cheers and is visibly moved, and even the tough judge acknowledges talent when confronted by it. Whether or not these singers win the competition or are displaced by the end, the larger narrative is clear. They have already won by overcoming odds and gaining the respect of the audience and judges who had previously underestimated, derided, and patronized them. The most famous example was probably Susan Boyle's audition in 2009 on *Britain's Got Talent*. She was preceded in 2007 by the unassuming mobile phone salesman Paul Potts who turned out to be a powerful operatic tenor. The story repeated itself with the duo "Jonathan and Charlotte" in 2012. The shy and overweight Jonathan turned out to possess what a judge called one of the best opera voices he had heard in years.

I wonder about the appeal of this scenario in which the plain duckling turns out to have a gorgeous voice. I do not think that we can attribute it merely to sexism or that it is particular to fans of certain musical genres, as the scenario has been played out with both men and women and across a number of different musical genres. To give another example, in 2009 Kevin Skinner, an unprepossessing country singer and "former chicken catcher," belied his unsophisticated appearance with a heartfelt and polished performance and went on to win *American Idol*.

Why do we presume that a beautiful voice (which is, after all, a natural gift), must necessarily exist together with the natural gifts of physical beauty and grace? And why do we assume that vocal expression (after all, a learned skill), should not be equally accessible to the gorgeous and the plain? Unfortunately, I do not know the answers to these questions.

A Tension in Singing

Musicians are more than conduits. One may say, "I'm listening to Beethoven's Pastoral Symphony," but what one actually listens to is a particular performance or a recording of a particular performance. All music intended for performance (as opposed to playback through electronic instruments) must be performed before it can be heard. And when musicians perform, they shape the music we hear in various ways – whether through the timbre of their particular instruments, the physical space in which they play, or the nuances of rhythm, pitch, articulation, and phrasing in their interpretations. And what is true of instrumentalists is even more apposite of singers, because singers are not separate from their instruments. We do not hear "House of the Rising Sun"; rather, we hear the Animals perform it, or Bob

Dylan, or Nina Simone, or whomever is singing it this week on a TV talent search.

If we stop to think about it, we realize that singers must "put on a show." We seem to understand that singing is a performing art, and may recognize that it shares elements with acting. Yet there also seem to be limits to how far audiences are willing to follow singers. We do not accept just any song from any singer. This can make for a tension in the relationship between audiences and singers.

Some remarks by philosopher Suzanne Langer are helpful in understanding what I have identified as a "tension" between singers and audiences. In her discussion of musical performance Langer distinguishes between two forms of self-expression. First, there is self-expression such that the work is a vehicle for the performer's moods. Second, there is self-expression understood as "ardor for the impact conveyed."[13] This second form of self-expression is the performer's actual feeling, his "impassioned utterance" or contagious enthusiasm for the content of the work. This quality, Langer claims, belongs naturally to the human voice. However, the demands placed on the human voice when it is asked to perform in song are in conflict with its function as an instrument of biological response. She writes: " ... all actual emotions, crude or fine, deep or casual, are reflected in [the voice's] spontaneously variable tone. It is the prime avenue of self-expression, and in this demonstrative capacity not really a musical instrument at all."[14]

The tension between singers and audiences, then, reflects the tension between the voice as instrument of self-expression and the voice as musical instrument. Keith Richards describes this well when he reminisces about listening to the popular music of the early 1960s, in particular "Will You Love Me Tomorrow" by the Shirelles: "Shirele Owens, their lead singer, had an almost untrained voice, beautifully balanced with a fragility and simplicity, *almost as if she wasn't a singer*" (emphasis added).[15] The implication is that there is an inconsistency between "being a singer" – presumably, a professional singer – and the self-expression that is revealed in the qualities of fragility and simplicity in Owens' performance.

Yet, in all singing, elements of self-expression mix with elements of performance and it is difficult to imagine any singing that could be "purely" one or the other. Howls of grief and shrieks of joy are not songs, after all. There can be elements of performance in the most seemingly unselfconscious singing, and there can be elements of personal revelation, intended or not, in a polished or contrived performance.

Recognizing the tension between self-expression as revealing of the performer's mood and self-expression as "ardor for the impact conveyed" can help account both for the power of some of the best singers and for the lack of aesthetic appropriateness we sense when a singer chooses the wrong song. In some of the most effective and moving vocal performances, the voice as musical instrument overlaps nearly seamlessly with the voice as instrument of self-expression. Critic Alex Ross writes: "Some performers exert such a powerful presence – Billie Holiday, Sinatra, Elvis – that they seem to become the authors of songs that were actually the work of schlumpy men in the Brill Building."[16] I know exactly what he means. Johnny Cash's rendition of the song "I Hung My Head" on his *American IV: The Man Comes Around* is so authoritative that I have trouble accepting that he did not write it. (Readers will be able to supply their own examples.) When great performers sing the "right" songs there seems to be little gap between the voice as expressive of self and the voice as musical instrument. It is all too easy to believe that the song comes "straight from the heart," although the more sophisticated a listener, the more he is likely to be aware that professional singing is not mere self-expression. When singers choose the "wrong" song, the resulting incongruity thwarts our tendency to hear the human voice as a vehicle of self-expression.

"Love for Sale"

Like "My Heart Belongs to Daddy" and "Always True to You in My Fashion," "Love for Sale" is one of several songs with words and music by Cole Porter to explore the intersections of love and commerce. Originally written for the 1930 Broadway musical "The New Yorkers," the song is a first-person monologue by a prostitute and early recordings were banned from radio play. One contemporary reviewer wrote that the song was "in the worst possible taste" and another referred to it as a "threnody" – that is, a song of lamentation for the dead.[17] I can only assume that the reviewer was commenting on the elements of minor key tonality in the song. "Love for Sale" has been recorded many times since 1930, by singers and instrumentalists alike.

The words of the song are not euphemistic or coy; in fact the narrator sounds very matter-of-fact, as if she were selling any banal commodity. The cadence of the first iteration of the words "Love for sale" sounds to me reminiscent of a street seller's call. There were street sellers active in New York City until the end of World War II, so listeners at the time might well have made this connection. The impression that we're listening to a street caller is enhanced by the lyrics, "Who would like to sample my supply?"

Men who sing the song usually change the line "I go to work" to "She goes to work" if they sing the introduction, and they make other changes to put the song in the third person, rather than the first person. (So they sing about a prostitute, rather from the perspective of a prostitute.) The one exception I have come across (and there may be others) is the version by the Fine Young Cannibals who recorded the song in 1990 for the album *Red Hot + Blue*. This collection of Cole Porter songs recorded by various artists was conceived as a benefit for AIDS research.

While much could be said about "Love for Sale" from the perspective of gender and sexual orientation, I want to consider a different aspect of public persona: what listeners might be expected to know about a singer's life. Now, there may be people who listen to a recording, like it, yet care little or nothing about the person singing it and are not motivated to find out more about him or her. But I suspect that such people are in the minority. Typically, when we come across a performer whose work we appreciate, we want to know more. We may look for information on the internet, read the liner notes on CDs, seek out biographies and memoirs, etc. So, for the most part, I would venture, people who like a particular singer will know something about the broad outlines of his or her life. And this knowledge will influence how they hear that singer, and shape their responses to individual songs.

Billie Holiday and Ella Fitzgerald, two of the greatest female jazz vocalists of the twentieth century, recorded "Love for Sale" within a couple of years of one another: Holiday in 1954[18] and Fitzgerald in 1956.[19] Their renditions are quite different, and their very different personal histories affect how listeners today hear the two recordings. (I lack the imagination and historical knowledge to speculate on how the original audiences may have experienced these songs.)

Billie Holiday had a tragic life. Her health, compromised by drug and alcohol addiction, poverty, and association with violent men, was deteriorating by 1954. She would die five years later at the age of 44. Holiday's life was also marked by sexual violence. She was raped by a neighbor at age 11. Two years later, Holiday and her mother moved to Harlem in 1929 and both worked as prostitutes for several months. They were sent to prison when the brothel where they lived was raided by police.[20]

Ella Fitzgerald was two years younger than Holiday. While she also had personal setbacks and endured a period of homelessness as a teenager, her troubles were not in the same category as Holiday's, and not as widely publicized. Except for the occasional glass of champagne she didn't drink or use drugs. She was married for six years to the bass player Roy Brown, and they maintained amicable relations and continued to perform together after their divorce. In 1956, when she recorded *Ella Fitzgerald Sings the Cole Porter Songbook*, she was widely respected as a jazz innovator and arguably at the height of her powers. The titles of her "songbook" albums proclaim an equivalency of status between her and a number of highly acclaimed songwriters.

When Fitzgerald sings "Love for Sale," writes one reviewer, it "leaves you with the feeling that you have just heard another beautiful love song."[21] I think this remark is very apt. When I first heard the track (on an LP, in university) I was struck by the incongruity between the subject matter and Fitzgerald's polished performance. Fitzgerald sings the song beautifully and seemingly effortlessly, and without the note of "triumph" that I hear in some performances. The "knowing" (almost blasé) quality of her performance is enhanced by Buddy Bregman's very tasteful arrangement. She sounds a little world-weary, but not cynical. Nor does she sound sad, regretful, or like a woman who has really "been through the mill of love."

Holiday, on the other hand, sounds alternately sad and affectless. Hers is a very intimate performance, accompanied only by a piano. In the final iteration of the lyric "love for sale" which ends the song, her voice catches on the word "love" as if betraying the effort it has taken to sing the song. You believe it when she sings that she has "been through the mill of love" and she does not sing the line (as some do) as though it were something to be proud of.

Fitzgerald and Holiday were both great singers and I compare these recordings without the intention to rank order them. They have very different takes on the song, and I would submit that their contrasting performances are excellent in different ways. Knowing something of Holiday's life story, I cannot help but "hear" that past history in her performance. I do not mean to suggest that Holiday must have drawn on her life experiences when singing the song. She may or may not have done so. The creative process is mysterious and unless a performer is willing to share it, no one can pretend to know where a performative interpretation might come from. Rather, I am making a claim about listeners and about listeners' experience. Once we know something of the lives of Holiday and Fitzgerald, we will tend to hear their performances as reflecting what we know of their life histories. We may do this for no deeper reason than the tendency to confirmation bias – that is, the tendency we have to seek out information that confirms what we already believe rather than what refutes it.

In this chapter, I have tried to shed some light on the relationship between singers and audiences. I argued that audiences have expectations regarding which songs are appropriate for which singers, partly based on considerations of public persona. Audiences also have expectations concerning singers' attitudes to the songs they sing, and many of the expectations invoke the troubled concept of "authenticity." In the following two chapters, I take a closer look.

Notes

1 This question was put to him by (among others) Michael Spector in *The New Yorker* (September 9, 2002), hardly an unsophisticated source. Combs' reply provides the epigraph of this chapter.
2 Jan Swafford, "Nature's Rejects: The Music of the Castrati," *Slate,* November 9, 2009. www.slate.com/articles/arts/music_box/2009/11/natures_rejects.html (accessed December 9, 2014).
3 Godlovitch, *Musical Performance*, 13.
4 Godlovitch, *Musical Performance*, 50.
5 Godlovitch, *Musical Performance*, 50.
6 Godlovitch, *Musical Performance*, 142.
7 Godlovitch, *Musical Performance*, 139.
8 Godlovitch, *Musical Performance*, 143.
9 Theodore Gracyk, *I Wanna Be Me: Rock Music and the Politics of Identity* (Philadelphia: Temple University Press, 2001), 181.
10 John Seabrook, "The Money Note," *The New Yorker,* July 7, 2003, 53.

11 Richards, *Life*, 72.
12 Some findings are summarized in Nancy Etcoff, *Survival of the Prettiest: The Science of Beauty* (New York: Anchor Books, 1999).
13 Suzanne Langer, *Feeling and Form: A Theory of Art* (New York: Scribner, 1953), 141.
14 Langer, *Feeling and Form*, 141.
15 Richards, *Life*, 151.
16 Alex Ross, "Rock 101," *The New Yorker*, July 14, July 21, 2003, 92.
17 Both remarks quoted in www.jazzstandards.com/compositions-0/loveforsale.htm (accessed May 20, 2014).
18 http://youtu.be/V5nXmVkPPh8 (accessed May 18, 2014).
19 http://youtu.be/KeKLo10lwrI (accessed May 18, 2014).
20 The source is Stuart Nicholson, *Billie Holiday* (London: Victor Gollancz, 1995), 25 and 32–33.
21 www.jazzstandards.com/compositions-0/loveforsale.htm (accessed May 20, 2014).

5 Three Ways to Think about Authenticity in Performance

A voice is not like an oboe or violin, something you can take out of its case and put away

(John Potter – singer and academic)[1]

I have a friend who is a professional art appraiser. People consult her when they want to know the financial value of a painting or other artwork that they own. They may want to know this simply out of curiosity, or because they are considering selling it, or because they want to make sure that they have adequate insurance coverage. The issue of a work's authenticity or inauthenticity is important in my friend's appraisals. An authentic Modigliani – one actually painted by the artist – is worth far more than a copy of a Modigliani. Philosophers can discuss the aesthetic value of forgeries, and the different kinds of experience offered by original works and forgeries, and they can question whether our attitudes to forgeries and copies are strictly rational. But most of the time, these subtleties matter little to my friend or to her clients. For them, whether a work is authentic or not is a question of fact, and one that may have significant financial implications.

This kind of authenticity – whether an artwork truly came from the hand of a particular artist – arises in music relatively rarely. Yet "authenticity" is an important consideration for many listeners. When listeners fail to be convinced by a performance they sometimes express their disappointment in terms of the artist's authenticity or lack of the same. And while it may not be obvious at first, fans of diverse musical genres share concerns about singers' authenticity, although these concerns are likely to be expressed in different ways. This is not to say that concerns about authenticity are evenly distributed. Fans of some genres may care more than fans of other genres, and they are also likely to conceive of authenticity in different ways. We'll also see that concerns about authenticity in music may be the surface expression of deeper concerns about cultural appropriation and group identity.

In an earlier chapter I argued against some forms of aesthetic relativism. I claimed that disagreements regarding who is a "good singer" did not imply that there was no fact of the matter and no way to decide such questions. I suggested that we need to pay attention to broad agreement and consensus about such matters, as much as to controversy and disagreement. I will revisit some of these issues later in this chapter. Is there a fact about which singers are authentic and which are not? How do we decide these questions?

Before proceeding, I want to set aside another kind of authenticity in music that I won't discuss here. This is the question of whether an instance of a work faithfully reproduces the work's constituent properties. This type of authenticity is a matter of ontology, rather than of interpretation or the "politics" of performance.[2] Stephen Davies takes this ontological sense of authenticity to be its primary meaning, and, in declining to discuss it, I fear that I may be asked to turn in my "philosopher of music" credentials. I will take the risk. While the ontological issues Davies identifies are certainly interesting, especially with regard to Western classical music, I want to stay focused here on the meaning of authenticity for listeners and the role that perceptions of it might have in listeners' expectations and experience.

Concerns about authenticity are expressed in different ways by fans of different musical genres. I see three kinds of worries around authenticity: concerns about faithfulness to composers' intentions (almost exclusively the province of opera and art song); concerns about emotional expression; and concerns about maintaining boundaries.

Authenticity as Faithfulness (I)

Concerns with authenticity among fans of opera and art song revolve around what Peter Kivy calls "authenticity as intention," by which he means faithfulness to the *composer's* intentions.[3] We saw the composer Edward Cone in the previous chapter express a concern with this kind of authenticity, where he says that an "illegitimate" vocal interpretation is one in which the singer (rather than the vocal persona) is seen as embodying and "composing" the song that she sings. So in an illegitimate interpretation of, for example, Schubert's *Erlkönig*, instead of hearing the words as sung by each of the four characters, we would hear the voice of, say, Dietrich Fischer-Dieskau as though *he* was telling the story *in propria persona*.

It is not only composers who are worried about this kind of authenticity. Opera and art song singers are criticized for performing in a way that is "ego-driven"; in other words, in a manner insufficiently self-effacing towards the musical material. We can see this when we examine articles about opera and art song singers in the mass media. Music journalists (presumably reflecting concerns of the audience) frequently assure readers that the singers they profile are down-to-earth (rather than full of themselves) and that (perhaps consequently) their performances are not ego-driven either. So Dawn Upshaw appears "sensibly swathed in a duffel coat" (rather than a ball gown?) and doesn't "look like" an opera singer or think of herself as one. Because she is "anchored to the earth" her vocal flights above it are "wondrous."[4] Ian Bostridge is described as greeting the journalist at the door "brandishing hands caked with food" as he prepares lunch for his two children.[5] Another journalist reminds us that Lorraine Hunt Lieberson began her musical career as a viola player and developed as a musician in the (unglamorous) "inner voices" of the orchestra: "Perhaps as a result, her singing was never ostentatious or ego-driven, and always in service to the demands of the score and ensemble."[6] And to cite one more example, a recent profile of soprano Anna Netrebko tells us that she loves to party and shop (just like other women her age, it is implied) and that during her student days worked in the decidedly un-diva-like job as a janitor at St. Petersburg's Mariinsky Theatre.[7]

Now, music journalists may present these singers as "just ordinary folks" in an attempt to demystify opera and art song, which are often seen as elitist and difficult. And I don't mean to suggest that these kinds of singers are always presented as down-to-earth. Reports about another Russian soprano, Marina Poplavskaya, tend to stress rather than to down-play her difficult and "diva-like" behavior.[8] But the theme of "these world-class artists are just like you and me" comes up frequently enough to be of note. These portraits are not necessarily false but they are certainly selective. I think that at least one function of these portrayals – both the singers' self-presentation as down-to-earth and the journalists' reporting of it – is to reassure fans that singers are "authentic," in the sense of having sufficient respect for the music they perform to submerge their own egos in it. A certain way of being (down-to-earth, without pretensions, even ordinary) is seen as consistent with an approach to music that is also not showy.

Opera and art singers present themselves as serious musicians in the sense of taking a respectful and self-effacing attitude to the music they perform. Unlike successful people in other fields and in other musical genres, their personal narratives rarely contain elements of worldly ambition or the drive to succeed. They present themselves as not motivated by fame or fortune. In fact, in reading journalistic accounts of these singers' careers, I was struck also by the trope of the "accidental career." Many of these world-class artists are presented as somehow having fallen into vocal music. Hunt Lieberson turned to singing only after her viola was stolen; Netrebko originally wanted to be an actress; Bostridge started out as a historian. Although these singers have to train their voices, practice, learn new music, etc., we rarely hear about these components of their musical lives. Perhaps it would make for dull reading. Being a serious musician (something that is necessarily true of any even moderately successful singers in this genre) is reduced to only one of its many components: having a certain kind of attitude to the music, such that one is "authentic" in the right sense (i.e. humble) so as to sing it respectfully.

The Paradox of Performed "Authenticity"

"Authentic" is opposed to "fake" or "forgery" in the case of paintings and other works of art that are physically instantiated. Another sense of "authenticity" opposes it to insincerity. We contrast genuine or authentic sorrow with the pretense of sorrow and we usually recognize that emotional responses may be more or less genuine. We can usually recognize the difference between a genuine smile (what psychologists call a "Duchenne smile") and a fake smile. People may display less emotion than they feel (if they are stoic) or they may exaggerate their responses and come over as more angry or more pleased than they actually are. When a child or immature person expresses emotion beyond what a situation seems to indicate, we might say, "What a performance!" – meaning that we suspect some of the expressed emotion was feigned. Yes, the person was emotional and may have had good reason to be so, but something about their display of emotion struck us as overdone and therefore likely insincere and inauthentic.

A vocal music performance is a social interaction with a specific set of demands and expectations that vary according to culture and musical genre. Performers and audiences alike have roles to play and expectations to fulfill. Generally speaking, audiences recognize that a singer in performance is in the "performer" role. For example, singers and audiences are physically separated. Unless invited, audiences do not go on the stage to share the performance space. Listeners sing along with performers only in certain contexts, and usually only when encouraged to do so. Audience members do not usually comment on the performance in progress or initiate conversation with performers (although, depending on the type of performance, audience members may speak to one another). These are just some of the basic social conventions surrounding performance. Of course, these conventions are occasionally violated; however, if they break down completely the event in question is no longer a performance but something else.

Now here is the paradox: within the performance context, audiences (at least some audiences in some musical genres) desire and expect sincerity from performers, and they are disappointed to detect elements of insincerity. Why should this be so, given that everyone recognizes that a performance is a special kind of event, one that, by its very nature, has elements of artificiality? I think I have an answer to this question, which I will defer until we've delved a little deeper into authenticity.

Authenticity as Sincerity (II)

Authenticity is conceived of differently when we move from opera and art song to other music genres. In many forms of popular music, self-expression on the part of the performer is expected, so there are few worries about ego, "illegitimate" self-expression, or faithfulness to the composer's intentions. In jazz, blues, rock, and popular music, concerns about authenticity often take the form of worries about sincerity of emotional expression.

Singers in many musical genres make claims that the music they perform is important to them and that the emotion they convey in performance is genuinely felt. Although the following examples are drawn from interviews with jazz singers, I would bet that a survey of rock, hip-hop, or country singers would yield similar results.

So we have Diana Krall:

> I was watching Spalding Gray doing *Swimming to Cambodia* and I thought how wonderful it was that he took his life and made it art. I can't do that, but *all I can try to do is be myself,* even if sometimes the only people laughing are the guys on the bandstand.[9] (Emphasis added.)

So Krall does not "perform" (turn her life into art), so much as "be herself" on stage. In the same interview she also says that the choice of songs on the album she is currently promoting ("Glad Rag Doll") has personal resonance. It was inspired by compilation tapes that her father made for her when she was in music school. Dianne Reeves similarly mentions that the songs she sings have personal significance, and that she strives to sing them sincerely:

> A lot of the songs *took me back to a time of discovering who I was* [...] I feel like I am still courageous but I know now what I want. *Now I want to sing from a very clear place* because I see things and I have access to a broad array of information. I can speak about life now with some power.[10] (Emphasis added.)

Kurt Elling, speaking about the eclectic selection of songs he sings:

> I just try to do stuff *I can get behind emotionally* and believe.[11] (Emphasis added.)

Jazz singers present themselves as musicians whose work is personally and emotionally meaningful. I should acknowledge that this is not the only way in which they present themselves. Other themes that frequently arise in their interviews include their musical background and apprenticeship, expressions of gratitude to mentors and musical collaborators, and praise for past masters and sources of musical inspiration. Still, it is striking to me that jazz singers proclaim their sincerity as often as they do.

Remarks about sincerity and emotional authenticity from the mouths of jazz singers are particularly interesting because these singers do not typically write their own material but sing standards – songs written by others and often made famous by other performers. It would seem that popular music's "aesthetic of sincerity" is alive here as well. In making these claims singers reassure audiences of their sincerity, likely because they believe that their fans want or expect this kind of reassurance. Now, I do not mean to suggest that the sentiments are feigned. The point is that, by making such claims, singers are fulfilling a social role that they take to demand a certain attitude to their repertoire while meeting what they take to be the expectations of their fans.

Authenticity as Boundary Policing (III)

Jazz singing is also interesting for thinking about authenticity because, as one of the genres based on African-American musical traditions, questions of authenticity and singers' attitudes to the music they perform are entwined with issues of race and appropriation. Joel Rudinow's much-discussed paper, "Race, Ethnicity, Expressive Authenticity: Can White People Sing the Blues?"[12] focuses on one genre but has relevance for other genres similarly derived from African-American music.

The subtitle of Rudinow's paper asks a question about boundaries. If white people are playing the music in question, is it really blues? The implication, of course, is that blues is authentically performed only by blacks. Rudinow frames the question as one of ethnicity. For other listeners, boundary questions about music may be framed in different ways. Keith Richards remembers intense debates about authenticity among blues fans in London in the early 1960s. He says that a group he calls the "blues purists" were "very stuffy and conservative, full of disapproval." While it was taken for granted that the performers of authentic blues were African-American, ethnicity was far from the only relevant factor for these fans. Richards recalls a Muddy Waters show in Manchester where Waters was virtually booed off the stage when he played a second set with an electric band. For this audience, Richards says, "blues was only blues if somebody got up there in a pair of old blue dungarees and sang about how his old lady left him. None of these blues purists could play anything. But their Negroes had to be dressed in overalls and go 'Yes'm boss.' And in actual fact they're city blokes who are so hip it's not true."[13] Richards' anecdote is illustrative of the different things that can matter to fans; not only ethnicity, but also elements of public persona and instrumentation can be taken as marking authenticity.

Blues, as it draws on folk traditions, may be particularly likely to arouse debates about authenticity among its fans. But such debates are actually ubiquitous in popular music. Is a singer too pop to be *really* country? Not gritty enough to be *genuine* punk? In fact, Jennifer C. Lena, a sociologist who studies popular music, has found that boundary-policing debates about authenticity have touched nearly every style of twentieth and twenty-first century music, from electronic dance to South Texas polka.[14]

How might we judge whether a particular performer is "authentic" in a particular genre? In his paper on the blues, Rudinow characterizes authenticity as the kind of credibility that comes from having the appropriate relationship to an original source.[15] He argues that the authenticity of a blues performance turns on the degree of mastery of the idiom rather than on the performer's ethnicity. Evidence of authenticity can be sought "in and around the performance" for the performer's recognition and acknowledgement of indebtedness to sources of inspiration and technique.[16] So, for Rudinow, authenticity is an objective matter, rather than a matter of subjective taste or opinion. One can make arguments that a particular musician has or has not mastered the idiom and therefore is or is not authentic. It seems plausible that Rudinow's claims could be extended to at least some other musical genres. So in judging if a hip-hop artist, say, is authentic, we might consider his mastery of the idiom (how well he raps, etc.) and whether he shows an understanding of hip-hop's history and past masters.

I value Rudinow's position because it acknowledges that there is more to music and to our experience of music than sound. A listener's judgment of vocalists' authenticity to a particular tradition may be based on how they sound, but they are also influenced by their public persona, including but going beyond those factors that Rudinow mentions. We can see this illustrated in the film *8 Mile* which starred and was based on the life of (white) rapper Eminem. The climax of the film is a "battle" (rapping contest) between Jimmy (the character played by Eminem) and a succession of African-American rappers, staged in front of a predominantly black audience. The film up to this point can be seen as making a case for the plausibility of Jimmy's victory. It is not just Jimmy's appropriate relationship to original sources that is seen as crucial, although the film takes care to make us aware of it. Just as importantly, we have seen Jimmy's difficult life, economic deprivation, hassles on the job, difficulty finding love, his pleasure and ability in rapping, and his close friendships with African-Americans. Even the title of the film is a marker of authenticity; it refers to Eight Mile Road, the border between the impoverished black city of Detroit and the wealthier white northern suburbs. In the rap which wins the final contest Jimmy taunts his black opponent with lacking the right kind of background despite being African-American – he comes from a loving suburban middle class family and has had the advantage of an elite private school education. The quality of the contestants' lived experience is important to the audience judging the rap contest. The implication is that it should be so for us too, and the film is as much an argument for Eminem's authenticity as it is for Jimmy's. (Yet I should add that not every viewer was so convinced. Elvis Mitchell, in reviewing *8 Mile* for the *New York Times* charged that, "the film embraces the absurdity of a white rapper who takes down a brother in a club full of black people – perhaps more black people than own Eminem records.")[17]

Twenty years have passed since the publication of Rudinow's seminal article. Does race still deserve consideration as a relevant boundary marker for authenticity of a blues performer? What about as an authenticity marker for other musical genres? Writing in 1999, Kembrew McLeod found that blackness was one (but not the only) marker of authenticity for fans of hip-hop.[18] More than 15 years later, some would go so far as to argue that North American society is now "post-racial," and that discussions of race have little place in thinking about current popular music. While I doubt this is true, I also do not feel that this is the right place (or I am the right person) to pursue that discussion.

To sum up: Fans of nearly every genre of popular music make boundary-policing arguments about singers. These arguments may be based on a number of factors, including sonic qualities of the music ("too pop"), accompanying instrumentation ("electric guitars don't belong in a blues performance"), a singer's public persona ("he's no gangsta"), and so on.

Authenticity clearly matters to fans, whether we are talking about expectations of sincerity, about boundary issues, or about the attitude that singers take to their repertoire. Why? In the following two sections I discuss two types of possible reasons. Both apply to musical performance in general, and the second is more relevant for singing.

Authenticity: Music and Group Identity

I began this chapter by telling you about my friend the art appraiser. In her work, authenticity is inherent in objects. A painting either originated from the hand of a particular artist or it did not. I said that this way of conceiving of authenticity has some relevance for music, but a much more potent concept of authenticity has to do with fans' expectations. I hinted that concerns about authenticity in music might be a way of talking about deeper issues, those having to do with cultural appropriation and group identity.

If authenticity is not inherent in an object or event, where is it? Here I follow the thinkers in a diverse number of fields who would argue that "authenticity" (and a number of other concepts) are socially constructed. Before saying much more, I want to disarm critics who might claim that "socially constructed" concepts are trivial or merely subjective or somehow "unreal." This line of criticism is simply mistaken. Take the laws of one's society, for example. These were socially constructed in the sense of being thought up and written down by people who came before us. Even if you believe that a nation's laws are divinely inspired, an element of social construction must enter when these laws are written down and again when they are interpreted. Laws continue to be socially modified as they are interpreted and adjusted by people today. Yet a society's laws are anything but trivial. Laws have real, measurable consequences and can exert a powerful effect on people's behavior. Furthermore, to acknowledge that a concept is socially constructed does not mean that it is "merely" socially constructed – that it has no basis in the external world. Race and gender are both powerful socially constructed concepts with a basis in human biology. The crucial point is that neither can be *reduced* to human biology. There is more to gender than biological sex and more to race than physical characteristics or DNA sequences.

So in claiming that authenticity is socially constructed by communities of musical fans, I do not mean to denigrate its importance or its ontological status. I recognize that authenticity claims are profoundly important to some fans. What I want to explore in this section and the next are some of the reasons *why* they might be important.

Again, I find Lena's work on authenticity in popular music to be really useful here.[19] She has found that most major musical styles have followed a similar trajectory. They begin with an "avant-garde" phase that is driven by musicians who come together to jam, share recordings, and bemoan the state of current popular music. If they keep at it long enough, they develop what she calls a "scene." They converge on a style, perform in public, and start to develop a fan base. If the music becomes better known and of wider interest (if there is a "buzz" around it) then the next stage – the "industry-based" phase – might begin. With this stage comes national attention, an influx of cash, and media hype. Debates over authenticity are almost always triggered by this phase – when the scene is "threatened" by the music industry's attention – and they become more frequent and intense from there. Eventually, if a style becomes more firmly established, concerns about authenticity fade. Some musical genres go on to exhibit a fourth "traditionalist" phase when some fans and musicians push for the preservation and celebration of the pre-industry phases.

One of Lena's central examples is the authenticity debates among hip-hop fans. "Rapper's Delight" by the Sugarhill Gang was the first release that took the emerging musical style out of the Bronx where it began and into mainstream culture. Along with national media attention, the single started debates over what counted as "genuine" hip-hop. (Some hip-hop fans in the Bronx claimed never to have heard of the Sugarhill Gang before it won national success.) Debates over authenticity have been reflected in the changing content of rap lyrics over the past years. Lena writes: "In the early years, the music was produced mainly by independent record labels, and the lyrics focused on whatever mattered to the kids writing the songs, like partying, romance, or competition between dueling bands in the scene. In 1988, however, soon after the major record labels took over the rap market, lyrics took a dramatic turn toward boasts of street credibility voiced by an array of 'hustler' protagonists. Just when the industry passed fully into corporate hands, its lyrical currency shifted to favor competitive claims of gritty authenticity."

Hip-hop's trajectory is fairly typical, and Lena tells a similar story about Seattle grunge rock. As she demonstrates, conversations about authenticity become particularly intense when a musical sub-culture is seen as under threat from corrupting outside influences. Boundary debates over musical styles tend to focus on qualities of the music in question, but they are rarely *only* about music. Rather they are a way of making larger claims about who belongs and who doesn't. As Lena puts it, "fundamental questions of group identity hang in the balance."

People preserve their culture by attempting to draw boundaries around it. Among other things, belonging to a national, ethnic or religious group can mean eating this (but not that), speaking in this way (but not that way), or celebrating this holiday (but not that one.) These are just some of the ways in which people have "fenced off" their identity as (say) Canadian or African-

American or Jewish or whatever. Listening to certain kinds of music and singing certain kinds of songs (but not others) is another way of reinforcing boundaries around group identity. National anthems are the most obvious example, but by no means the only one. Music can create and reinforce personal and social identity on a smaller level as well. Many music fans, especially adolescents, identify strongly with their preferred style of music. Probably most of us have felt that instant sense of fellowship that arises when we find that a recent acquaintance likes the same kind of music that we do. We may have also experienced the fellowship that arises when we find that another person *dislikes* the same music that we do.

Debates about authenticity are important to fans when music (this music, but not that music) is constitutive of personal or social identity. Boundary-policing conversations about music are a way of staking out one's identity and drawing boundaries around one's culture or sub-culture. Fans demonstrate expert familiarity with a style to other fans in the community when they can make increasingly fine distinctions about what properly belongs to that style and what doesn't. Discussion – even disagreements – are a way of connecting with others, as only those who care deeply about a musical style will bother to argue about it.

Authenticity: Singing Is Personal

I have been making the case that "boundary debates" about musical styles have a strongly social aspect. I think that the same is true for the other kind of authenticity – the claim that a performer is or is not sincere.

I have argued at length elsewhere that all musical experience is intrinsically and fundamentally social rather than personal or individual.[20] The way that I understand music, even listening on headphones alone in a room is a social experience, through and through. Music's social character can be seen in the role it plays in every culture – past and present – in creating and reinforcing social bonds, whether these are bonds between caregivers and infants, adult partners, friends, or among members of social groups and sub-groups. Music is typically made in interaction with others, with a score coded by others or according to traditions developed by others, with instruments made by others. Even a seemingly individualistic experience of music is derivative, secondary, and carries a social meaning. If a musician were to make her own instrument, compose or improvise her own music, and decline to play in front of others, then we might say that her music-making was an individual activity. However, what she did would be understandable as "music" only if we could connect her actions to some larger musical practice.

What holds true about the social character of music is, if anything, true in a more fundamental way for singing. Singing is a form of interpersonal communication. Because its medium is the human voice and because the voice invokes the human and therefore the social, a song can feel like a personal communication, even when the listener is just one of many in a crowd. Insincere communication – or communication that is perceived by the recipient to be insincere – damages relations between people. The insincere apology, the disingenuous compliment, the reluctantly given invitation – all of these can be a source of tension between people and can end relationships.

Reciprocity – understood as treating others in a way commensurate with how they have treated us, and expecting others to treat us as we have treated them – is a powerful social norm. When fans sincerely feel enthusiasm and affection for performers and music, it is only natural that they want these emotions to be reciprocated in a genuine way. They want to feel that the singers they admire are just as eager to perform for them as they are to listen. They do not want to feel that performers are just "doing their job" or "in it for the money." Hence the expectation that singers be authentic in the sense of "performing" sincerity effectively. As an audience, we want to be the recipient of a sincere communication.

I suspect that our more rational selves know (or should know) that singers and other performers cannot possibly feel all of the emotions they project in performance, each and every time they perform. If singers did in fact experience all of the emotions that they must project, their work would be too difficult and draining. Yet at another level, we want to feel that singers are performing in a genuine way and conveying something true of their own lives and experience. Hence the importance of a singer's public persona. Sometimes the persona can do part of the work of conveying a singer's lived experience, and, when fans are familiar with the persona, it informs their perception and understanding of the singer's performances.

Authenticity: Is It All Subjective? How to Decide?

Earlier I proposed that "authenticity" is not inherent in performances but is socially constructed. Now, this does not imply that all claims about performers' authenticity are merely subjective. Things are more complicated, and much depends on what a person is trying to say when he or she claims that a performer or performance is or is not authentic.

Some authenticity claims purport to be claims of fact. In their book *Faking It: The Quest for Authenticity in Popular Music*, Hugh Barker and Yuval Taylor devote a chapter to the career and reception of Mississippi John Hurt (approx. 1892–1966).[21] Hurt was a sharecropper who played guitar and sang at local parties and dances and recorded a few songs with Okeh Records in 1928. These were commercial failures and Hurt soon returned to obscurity. In 1963 a musicologist rediscovered Hurt and helped him to revive his career. Hurt performed extensively until his death and was heralded as an authentic blues performer. The reality was more complicated, as Hurt did not actually meet some of the standard criteria of a blues singer, and much of the music he played was contemporary popular music with little blues influence.

Many of Hurt's fans were drawn to his music because of its purported authenticity and the connections it seemed to offer to a simpler past (and some just liked his guitar playing). Some may have been motivated in perhaps subtle ways by racist beliefs about African-American music – much like the British fans Richards remembers who thought that blues performers must be unsophisticated bumpkins. If these fans were to insist on Hurt's authenticity – and if by that, they meant his status as an old-time bluesman – then they would be mistaken. Hurt came to the blues quite late in his career. So if fans meant to make a claim about a matter of ethnomusicology or musical historiography, then these claims should be assessed for their truth value by the relevant experts.

If authenticity claims are judgments about an artist's place in a musical tradition, they come close to the kind of authenticity that is the concern of my art appraiser friend. In this kind of case, experts in that musical tradition get to decide if these claims are true or not. This is not to say that experts will always necessarily agree, any more than my friend will always come to the same conclusion as another art appraiser. Indeed, experts may disagree and they may talk past one another if there is underlying controversy about the characteristics and defining features of different musical styles. I should note that experts in a musical style may or may not be fans of that style, and fans may or may not be experts.

At the same time, I think that Barker and Tayor may have misunderstood some of the fans' responses to Hurt. Claims about performers' authenticity are not always claims about music history and traditions. Sometimes "authentic" is playing a different kind of role. Let me quote Richards again. Here he contrasts himself and Mick Jagger with the British "blues purists" who couldn't play any instruments and who had very rigid ideas about what was or wasn't genuine. He and Jagger also cared about authenticity, but they defined it differently:

> We'd hear something, we'd both look at each other at once. Everything was to do with sound. We'd hear a record and go, That's wrong. That's faking. *That's* real. It was either that's the shit or that isn't the shit, no matter what kind of music you were talking about. I really liked some pop music if it was the shit. But there was a definite line of what was the shit and what wasn't the shit. Very strict.[22]

Richards makes some attempts at clarifying what he means by "real." "I was looking for the core of it," he says, "the expression." He discusses different blues styles and techniques, and also repeats how he loves some pop music. But although Richards is expressing himself in the language of authenticity ("real," "faking") and boundaries ("a definite line"), I cannot help but think that he is actually saying something like "I like this music and not that music." "This music is real" (or "the shit") becomes another way of saying "This is my kind of music."

I suspect that Richards is not alone in using authenticity claims as a kind of short-hand for personal taste and strong conviction. When authenticity claims are disguised statements of musical taste, the person making the claim is the arbitrator of its truth. Generally speaking, I do not think that people can be mistaken about what they like and dislike, and arguments over such matters are a misplaced effort. There can be productive arguments over whether Mississippi John Hurt is an "authentic" bluesman or not, and about the relevant criteria for judging this question. But I doubt that one person can convince another, through argument, that he or she should enjoy Hurt's music. Arguments can convince someone to listen (or to listen again), and arguments can guide listening and single out different aspects of the music for closer attention. But the verbal arguments do only part of the work – the heavy lifting is done by perception.

Finally, I argued above that boundary-policing authenticity claims reflect concerns about community. It matters to fans whether a particular artist or a particular sound is truly authentic to a genre because such boundary-policing conversations about music are rarely *just* about music. They are a way of staking out one's identity and drawing boundaries around one's culture or sub-culture. And despite the philosophical shortcomings and potential confusion inherent in the language of authenticity, I don't see that it is likely to change or that there would be much point in encouraging reform. The notion of authenticity or "keepin' it real" is likely to remain part of the discourse of popular musicians and their fans.

When authenticity claims are claims about what belongs to a genre and what doesn't, fans of that genre are the ones who get to decide if the claims are true or not. This kind of authenticity makes sense only within a social group for whom the boundaries are important. They are the ones in a position to pronounce on questions surrounding it. For example, I enjoy some hip-hop, but I don't count myself a true fan. I know a little about the history of hip-hop and I follow some current discussions of it in the media (such as Questlove's series on the future of hip-hop in the on-line publication *Vulture*.)[23] I know what I like, but the music is not important enough to me for me to make claims about what is real or fake. Hip-hop is one of many musical genres I can enjoy; it isn't part of my identity. I'm not the one who should be adjudicating claims about which artists are authentic or not, or making meta-claims regarding what counts as authenticity in hip-hop. These matters are best left to fans. They are the ones who care about whether, say, Eminem or Insane Clown Posse or P.M. Dawn are truly authentic.

"Blues in the Night"

This song and the film in which it first appeared raise a host of issues related to authenticity, and attempting to think through them reveals just how complex and twisted these issues can be.

Let's start with the song as it is presented in the film.[24] Jigger (a jazz pianist), Nicky, and Peppi (two accompanying musicians) are thrown in jail after a fight breaks out in the St. Louis club where they have been performing. In the cell they meet one of Jigger's old friends, a bass player. The four discuss starting a band where they can play "real blues – that comes out of people's hearts." Peppi pleads with Jigger to start such a band then nearly faints after a fit of coughing. The cell opposite holds a group of African-American prisoners. They look alarmed and concerned by Peppi's coughing, and one calls out, "What's wrong with that white boy?" He continues: "He's got the miseries! We all got the miseries in here!" After this expression of racial solidarity, the camera pans to the other end of the cell where an African-American prisoner starts to sing "Blues in the Night." The other black prisoners provide unobtrusive backing vocals with elements of call and response. (For example, after the opening line, "My Momma done told me," one counters, "What'd she say?") The un-credited William Gillespie sings mournfully, with great expression, and incorporates melisma into his performance.

Meanwhile, Jigger and his friends hear the song and move from the back of their cell to the front in order to hear better. This exchange follows:

JIGGER: You hear that Peppi? It's great!

PEPPI: It sure is, Jigger.

JIGGER: That's the real misery, ain't it boys?

PEPPI: You could sure beat that out, couldn't ya, Jigger? [Meaning: Play it on a piano.]

ANOTHER: We all could

JIGGER: We all will! Boy, that's the blues – the real low-down New Orleans blues!

For the final verses of the song, presumably to stress the music's authentic origins, the film cuts to a montage of African-Americans doing physical work – picking cotton, moving cotton bales, unloading watermelons from a truck, etc. The montage ends with a close-up of a map with a route to New Orleans. Ironically, though the visuals are of African-Americans, the accompanying voices seem to belong to the film's white protagonists, singing in unison.

This short scene and the events leading up to it convey the following themes: (1) authentic or "real" music originates in human emotion, it "comes out of people's hearts"; (2) African-American music is authentic, and its authenticity is linked with the experience and the suffering of the people who sing and play it; (3) African-American music is worth imitating and (despite its roots in black experience) can be successfully imitated by whites. Jigger and his friends go on to form a jazz band and to perform the song "Blues in the Night" that they first heard from the black prisoner. The same point is made in another scene. Jigger and his friends meet Leo, a trumpet player. When Leo wants to show them that he's good enough to join their band, he stands up in a New Orleans club where they are having a meal and (uninvited) plays a solo with the African-American band onstage. Far from being put out, the black musicians welcome his contribution. I think that the message we're supposed to take from the scene is that white musicians, if they play well enough, can gain the respect of black musicians. If the African-American musicians think Leo is good enough to sit in with them, then the white musicians should be happy to have him; and (4) the film also conveys the theme that commercially popular music is inauthentic and performing it is a form of selling out. Jigger leaves his friends to earn a higher salary playing with "Guy Heiser's Band" in New York City. These white musicians (who wear bright white suits on stage) perform with the novelty singer "Baby Beth Barton" (the un-credited Mabel Todd) and their performance is presented as risible (if not the stuff of nightmares). The experience of playing with the group is seen as contributing to Jigger's eventual break-down. He is redeemed only by rejoining his friends and again playing "real" music.

Of course, "Blues in the Night" is not "found" music improvised by African-American prisoners. It was composed for the film by Johnny Mercer and Harold Arlen and has become part of the "Great American Songbook." Arlen intended the melody to sound like a blues folk song, and Mercer drew on his experiences living in the south among African-Americans to compose the lyrics. How are we to judge the song's "authenticity" according to the three ways that I have proposed?

The first form of authenticity – that of faithfulness to the composer's intentions – seems not to apply. In the film itself, the song is already taken out of its (faux) folk origins and played as an up-tempo number by Jigger's band. Later Jigger uses the melody to compose an ambitious piano piece in the mode of Gershwin's *Rhapsody in Blue*. Clearly, Arlen and Mercer did not intend "Blues in the Night" to be performed in one specific way. They were commercial songwriters whose livelihoods depending on their music gaining popularity and being performed widely.

What of authenticity in the second sense – that of the performers' sincerity? In the film Gillespie sings in character, and his character certainly seems to sing with sincere expression. Interestingly, later singers often undercut the sadness and pessimism of the lyrics by taking the song rather briskly and do not express much sadness. In short, they have fun with the song. Ella Fitzgerald, Cab Calloway, Louis Armstrong, and Tony Bennett, among others, sing the song in this way. One notable exception is Frank Sinatra, who recorded the song for his 1958 album *Only the Lonely* and sings it slowly and sadly. Yet all of these performers seem to be sincere in the sense of "sincerely wanting to give the audience a good experience." For example, Cab Calloway's exaggerated facial expressions, mugging, and rather obvious physical gestures (holding up two fingers for "a woman's a two-faced, a worrisome thing" and four fingers for "four winds") may have had an element of irony or satire, but they were clearly meant to engage the audience.

The third form of authenticity is authenticity to a particular musical genre, as determined by the community of fans. It might seem perverse to discuss the authenticity of "Blues in the Night" because no one (as far as I know) would claim it as genuine blues, in the sense of being a blues folk song. But other songs are readily characterized as "blues" despite not being the work of folk artists. I find it interesting to compare "Blues in the Night" with the song "Everyday I Have the Blues" attributed to Pinetop Sparks in 1935 and later reworked by Memphis Slim. Like "Blues in the Night," this song has been performed by many musicians, black and white, often as an up-tempo number that belies the sad and pessimistic lyrics. Are both songs "authentic"? Is neither? It depends whom we ask and what we mean by "authenticity." If we are asking about the songs' place in the American musical tradition, we should ask experts in the history of American music. We would expect them to provide criteria for what is to count as "authentic" blues and reasons for including or excluding each of the songs. If our question about authenticity is really a question about community, then we have to consult that community, and the inclusion of either song is not likely to be a pressing matter for any contemporary group. In the end, I would argue that the long-standing popularity of both songs among musicians and their evident respect for the songs make further questions about authenticity moot.

Notes

1 John Potter, "Introduction," *The Cambridge Companion to Singing* (Cambridge: Cambridge University Press, 2000), 1.
2 Davies, *Musical Works and Performances*, 227.
3 Peter Kivy, *Authenticities: Philosophical Reflections on Musical Performance* (Ithaca: Cornell University Press, 1995), 9–46.
4 Peter Conrad, "Dawn Chorus," *The Observer*, March 16, 2008, www.theguardian.com/music/2008/mar/16/classicalmusicandopera.review (accessed December 9, 2014).
5 Andrew Clark, "Heart and Head," *Financial Times*, May 27, 2011, www.ft.com/intl/cms/s/2/c1907796-87e5-11e0-a6de-00144feabdc0.html#ixzz30D8bujeB (accessed April 28, 2014).
6 Charlotte Higgins, "Obituary: Lorraine Hunt Lieberson," *The Guardian,* July 6, 2006, www.theguardian.com/news/2006/jul/06/guardianobituaries.usa (accessed December 9, 2014).
7 Charles McGrath, "A New Kind of Diva," *The New York Times,* December 2, 2007, www.nytimes.com/2007/12/02/magazine/02netrebko-t.html?ei=5087&em=&en=99d9474a7b50fc25&ex=1196830800&pagewanted=all (accessed December 9, 2014).
8 See Gay Talese, "Travels with a Diva," *The New Yorker,* December 6, 2010, 62–69.
9 Richard Ouzounian, "Diana Krall Says She's Given up Trying to Be a Diva," *Toronto Star,* February 15, 2013, www.thestar.com/entertainment/stage/2013/02/15/diana_krall_at_massey_hall_feb_21_and_22.html (accessed December 9, 2014).
10 Peter "Souleo" Wright, "After Deaths, Dianne Reeves Finds a Beautiful Life," *The Huffington Post*, February 14, 2014, www.huffingtonpost.com/peter-souleo-wright/on-the-a-wsouleo-after-de_b_4787954.html (accessed December 9, 2014).

11 Ted Panken, "Kurt Elling: 'You Can Feel When It Works'," *Downbeat*, December 2013. Archived at http://kurtelling.com/news/press_article_851.php (accessed December 9, 2014).

12 *Journal of Aesthetics and Art Criticism* 52:1 (1994), 127–37.

13 Richards, *Life*, 82–83.

14 Jennifer C. Lena, "Why Hipsters Hate on Lana Del Rey," *Pacific Standard*, December 19, 2012, www.psmag.com/navigation/books-and-culture/lana-del-rey-hip-hop-grunge-rick-ross-authentic-music-50442/ (accessed December 9, 2014).

15 Rudinow, "Race, Ethnicity, Expressive Authenticity," 129.

16 Rudinow, "Race, Ethnicity, Expressive Authenticity," 135.

17 See Elvis Mitchell's review in *The New York Times*, November 8, 2002.

18 Kembrew McLeod, "Authenticity within Hip-Hop and Other Cultures Threatened with Assimilation," *Journal of Communication* 49:4 (1999), 134–50.

19 Lena, "Why Hipsters Hate on Lana Del Rey."

20 Jeanette Bicknell, *Why Music Moves Us* (Basingstoke: Palgrave, 2009).

21 Hugh Barker and Yuval Taylor, *Faking It: The Quest for Authenticity in Popular Music* (New York: W.W. Norton & Co., 2007).

22 Richards, *Life*, 84.

23 Questlove, "When the People Cheer: How Hip-Hop Failed Black America," *Vulture*, April 22, 2014, www.vulture.com/2014/04/questlove-on-how-hip-hop-failed-black-america.html (accessed December 9, 2014).

24 *Blues in the Night*, dir. Litvak. 1941.

6   Authenticity, Value, and Technology

I began the previous chapter by telling you about my friend the art apprai-ser. The kind of authenticity that she invokes in her work lies at one end of the spectrum of possible concerns about authenticity in the arts. We've seen that things are more complicated in music, and especially in music perfor-mance. The extreme kind of case – where one performer's work is falsely represented as the work of another – is relatively rare. I can think of only two recent cases. In 1990 the duo Milli Vanilli had their Grammy award for "Best New Artists" rescinded when it was revealed that they were not the singers on the debut album purported to be their work. This information came to light when, during a supposed live performance, their backing track skipped and it was revealed that they had been lip synching rather than singing. The second case was the scandal in 2007 when CDs purporting to be recordings of pianist Joyce Hatto were determined to be of other pianists.

The Hatto "forgeries" (perpetrated by her husband) and the Milli Vanilli deception were made possible by advanced recording technology. Auto-tune is another recent technology that raises issues pertaining to authenticity. Yet we'll see that the issues raised by Auto-tune go beyond those of authenticity, and that a concern for authenticity isn't necessarily the most fruitful way to think through the implications of the technology.

Auto-tune – Some Background

"Auto-tune" is the proprietary name for the pitch-correction software developed by Antares Audio Technologies. (Like "Kleenex" and "Xerox" before it, "Auto-tune" is a brand name well on the way to becoming a common noun.) The software adjusts pitch up or down to the nearest semi-tone so that performers can seem always to be hitting intended pitches, and it can be used for instruments as well as for voices. The first major com-mercial release to use Auto-tune was Cher's single "Believe" in 1998. Auto-tune can be used both in the recording studio and during live performance. In addition to its correction function, Auto-tune can also be used as a sound effect to make human voices sound artificial or manufactured. The deploy-ment of Auto-tune can be obvious and unintentionally make a singer sound robotic; however, if used sparingly and with subtlety, it can be difficult for listeners to detect.

I am old enough to remember the time before drum machines came to dominate popular music, and the advent of Auto-tune gives me a feeling of déjà vu. Both are technological innovations developed by parties other than performers (instrument makers and electronics innovators in the case of drum machines, and Andy Hildebrand, a research scientist and engineer, in the case of Auto-tune.) Both are used to imitate or "perfect" a human activity (maintaining a rhythmic pulse and singing in tune) as well as to create novel musical effects. Both are widely used (not to say ubiquitous) in some genres (drum machines in hip-hop and dance music and Auto-tune for much mainstream popular music) and little used in others (jazz, opera, and art music.) Both arouse strong feelings among proponents and detractors, and proponents of both claim that the technology saves time and money.

In a previous chapter I discussed Stan Godlovitch's account of musical performance. I have found his discussion of the institutional context of music-making to be helpful in thinking through the implications of Auto-tune, which, I will continue to suggest, have much in common with the implications aroused by drum machines. Godlovitch begins from the premise (uncontroversial, to my mind) that musical performance requires skill. Drawing an analogy with the medieval craftsmans' guilds that originated in the Middle Ages and controlled the practice of a craft in a particular area, Godlovitch argues that musical communities are also structured in guilds.[1]

Musicians' "guilds" are organized by instrument. One of their main functions, Godlovitch claims, is to maintain the craft's "skill-centered exclusivity." In other words, if someone does not have adequate skills of the right kind, he or she is not granted membership in the guild. For example, not just anyone who picks up a violin is considered a "violinist" – even an amateur violinist. Many people never progress past the stage of "student of the violin." Guilds establish membership credentials, regulate standards of proficiency, and ensure consistency in the recognition of merit. They also regulate innovations in instrument design and reject changes that would make the instrument in question too easy to play. If we look at the history of the development of the violin we find that some innovations have been accepted (steel or steel-wound strings instead of gut strings) but others were rejected (re-shaping the instrument so as to get one's hands around it more easily). A violin remains difficult to play with steel strings, but a re-shaped violin would make the instrument easier to play and therefore more widely accessible. Such modifications would diminish the level of skill required to play the violin and thereby threaten the guild's skill-centered exclusivity.

Clearly, both drum machines and Auto-tune democratize (or if you prefer, cheapen) skilled activities, and, in doing so, both have the potential to be disruptive innovations. Indeed, the wide use of drum machines has already put hundreds of live percussionists out of work.[2] I do not mean to imply that programming drum machines or the judicious use of Auto-tune are not skilled activities. The point is that they recruit *different* skills than do drumming or singing in tune. The percussion guild has not been able to halt the adoption of drum machines in the way that the violin guild was able, in the past, to regulate innovations to the violin. Perhaps this indicates that drum machines are a different instrument rather than an adaptation or innovation of traditional percussion instruments, despite their shared rhythmic function. There are indications that a drum machine/electronic music guild is forming that will regulate standards and maintain skill-centered exclusivity, much as the guilds for traditional instruments do. In that case, traditional percussionists who can also program drum machines might end up as members of both guilds.

Does it make sense to talk about a singers' guild, and what are the implications for thinking about Auto-tune? I see the strongest case for a singers' guild in the world of opera and art song where there are still significant barriers to entry. Performing in an opera is not a feasible "do-it-yourself" project. As yet there is no equivalent in the opera world to the garage band unknowns who can post on YouTube or MySpace and build a following through social media. The skills required to perform the operatic and art song repertoire – sound singing technique and breath control, the ability to read music and perhaps play an instrument, knowledge of foreign languages, musicality and (for opera) acting ability – mean that singers require training and support, usually in a formal setting. Formal institutions such as university music departments, conservatories, competitions, artist-in-residence programs, and the like can readily be seen as aspects of Godlovitch's guild scenario.

For other types of singing and other repertoires, on the other hand, the guild analogy is less persuasive. The world of popular singing is highly diffuse. There seems to be room for everyone from singers with a wide vocal range and admirable control (Steven Tyler of Aerosmith, Beyoncé, Whitney Houston), singers with relatively small ranges (Billie Holiday – less than two octaves,[3] Karen Carpenter – just over two octaves[4]), singers without a traditionally pleasing vocal tone (Leonard Cohen, Bob Dylan, Tom Waits), and singers who require significant studio enhancement (Britney Spears, Paula Abdul, Selena Gomez, and others). There are more ways of becoming a successful popular singer than there are of being a successful singer in the world of opera and art song. This aesthetic "democracy" – as well as the commercial pressures on popular music – weaken the forces that would maintain an exclusivity based on skill. Anyone can upload their performance to the internet and crowd-source funding for an album. In the end, though, the market decides who is a successful popular singer and who remains unknown or a local phenomenon. So while not anyone can just elect themselves to join the ranks of "popular singers," whether or not someone in fact succeeds in becoming a popular singer would seem to have little to do with their acceptance into a guild centered on the exclusivity of vocal skills.

Yet even with the diffuse nature of what I have called the world of popular singing, we see vestiges of a guild structure in the frequent appeal to
"community standards." The world of popular music may be diffuse and
may have different standards than the world of opera and art song, but it is
not anarchic. One prominent illustration can be found in Beyoncé's press
conference confessing that her singing of the American national anthem at
President Obama's 2012 inauguration was not in fact live. She listed the
barriers a live performance would have faced (bad weather, no time for a
sound check, insufficient time to rehearse with the orchestra) and said: "I
decided to sing along with my pre-recorded track – which is very common
in the music industry."[5] In other words, what she did at the inauguration
did not violate community standards.

It is important to remember that, in both the opera and the popular music
"communities," standards are not static but change over time. We can see
this in the opera world in the controversies over the use of microphones in
live performance. Traditionally, opera singers were expected to sing without
amplification. With the move to large outdoor venues, the use of microphones in such performance spaces became accepted. Now there is suspicion
that amplification is being used with weaker singers (those with "light"
voices) in prestigious indoor venues as well. (See, for example, the discussion on the "Opera Chic" blog about an incident at Madrid's Teatro Real.
There were shouts of "verguenza!" or "shame!" when some members of the
audience came to believe that singers Marco Vratogna and Fiorenza Cedo-
lins were singing with the aid of microphones.)[6] Perhaps standards will
change to the extent that microphones become the norm one day.

From my perspective, community standards regarding Auto-tune in popular
singing are also in flux. When Lessley Anderson was researching Auto-tune
for an article in *The Verge*, she found that few artists would admit to using
it. At the same time, producers and other industry insiders repeatedly told
her that "everyone" was using it. The only difference was that some were
using it more obviously and more frequently than others.[7] Like Beyoncé,
crooner and jazz singer Michael Bublé, who admitted to using Auto-tune on
his pop-crossover song "It's a Beautiful Day," justified his acceptance of the
technology through an appeal to community standards: "I need to get on
pop radio. And if my songs don't sound like all the other songs, I'm not
getting on pop radio."[8] (Although the track may have got Bublé on pop
radio, it sounds totally undistinguished and I doubt very much it won him
any new fans.)

To sum up: while it is still plausible to argue for the existence of a guild
structure in opera and art song, we now can see only vestiges of such a
structure in the world of popular singing. This is due to a number of reasons, including the historical development of recent popular music and the
commercial pressures it faces. Yet the idea of "community standards"
remains potent, and community standards concerning the use of Auto-tune
seem to be in flux. And as we saw in the previous chapter, the notions of

"authenticity" in music is closely tied to the expectations of a community – the community of fans.

Auto-tune and Authenticity

Twenty years after the Milli Vanilli incident, Fab Morvan, the surviving member of the duo, gave a wide-ranging interview to journalist Mike Hess. Among other topics, he had this to say about Auto-tune:

> I have to say something and be clear about it. When people say: "Well, you didn't sing on the record" ... OK, cool. I didn't. But to be technical, when someone records in a studio and Auto-Tune does your job, it isn't you anymore. It could be anyone, because you're not doing it anymore, the machine is doing it. So, are you doing it? When it comes time to perform it live, you can't replicate it. So when people say "You should sing on the record, man." Well, yeah, but now technically a lot of the people who are singing on the record with Auto-Tune aren't doing their job.[9]

In effect, Morvan claims here that use of Auto-tune is a kind of misrepresentation, and that it is not so very different from the misrepresentation he was involved in. I want to focus on two of the issues he raises: that Auto-tuned vocals are no longer truly representative of the singer ("it isn't you anymore") and that one key aesthetic (or perhaps even moral) issue is that the Auto-tuned singer cannot replicate his or her performance in a live setting.

Let's assume that Morvan is talking about the secret or surreptitious use of Auto-tune by a singer who would otherwise be noticeably off pitch. Is it correct to say that the Auto-tuned vocals are no longer representative of the singer? Much in the way that early photographers used the camera not simply to document the world "as is" but to create artistic effects, recording engineers have also experimented with ways of making musicians sound better or different since at least the commercial use of the technology. The resources of today's professional music studios (and even those within reach of non-professionals) are considerable. In addition to pitch correction there is added reverb, layering (or multi-tracking), dynamic range compression, and others. Auto-tune seems to be just the latest tool in the music producer's kit that makes recordings sound different (some would say better) than "straight" live recordings.

So the question becomes: once we have accepted all manner of recording studio effects, is Auto-tune a significant enough departure such that recordings that employ it are no longer representative of a singer? Are singers whose recordings use Auto-tune really like Milli Vanilli and Joyce Hatto, who had little or no involvement in the recordings issued in their names?

I do not have definitive answers to these questions. To my mind, they are not the sort of questions that have evident answers. One place to draw the line between acceptable enhancements and those that misrepresent the performer in question is where Morvan draws it. Can the performer replicate in a live setting what he or she seems to be able to do on a recording? Beyoncé implicitly appealed to this standard at the press conference I mentioned earlier. Before speaking about what had happened at the inauguration, she asked everyone present to stand and then sang "The Star Spangled Banner" (a notoriously difficult song for vocalists) live without accompaniment. It was her way of saying, "I'm a good singer. Don't misjudge me based on an isolated incident."

This answer has an intuitive appeal because it neatly specifies a clear criterion. Unfortunately, issues in philosophical aesthetics tend to be messy. First, no singer (and no musician) sings or plays exactly in tune on every occasion. Even the greatest have off-days. So now we have simply moved the criterion from "the singer must be able to sing in tune in a live setting" to "what rate of being off-pitch is acceptable?" I do not mean to imply that there is no answer to this question; rather, there is no evident, obvious answer that one can provide without argument or defense. Furthermore, a great deal of popular music is now a recording art as much as (or more than) it is a performing art. Many tracks either cannot be replicated on stage or need significant pre-recorded components to be replicated in a live setting. So we have the same problem we had when considering studio enhancements: where to draw the line between recording effects that are acceptable enhancements, and those that are deceptive? Must we do this on a case-by-case basis, or can we formulate and defend some general principles?

Proponents of Auto-tune reject the idea that its use is deceptive (or deceptive in a significant way). When Hildebrand is asked if his invention is "evil," his stock answer has been, "My wife wears make-up, does that make her evil?"[10] In other words, Auto-tune is an acceptable enhancement and worries about it are misplaced. We don't take the position that a woman wearing lipstick is doing anything untoward. She's simply trying to put her "best" self on display, sometimes in response to community standards. Unlike plastic surgery, the use of make-up does not alter appearances in a fundamental way. A woman who wears lipstick is not in disguise and does not misrepresent herself.

While I don't think that Auto-tune is necessarily "evil," neither do I find it as innocuous as make-up. Being physically attractive is a natural gift; singing in tune is a learned skill. I care about what a singer really sounds like and what he or she is genuinely capable of, in a way that I don't care about what people really look like without make-up or other enhancements. I would feel deceived if I formed an erroneous impression about a singer's skill based on an Auto-tuned performance. It seems far better to tolerate a few off-key pitches. But at the same time, I realize that my preferences may not be shared by others. As Auto-tuned vocals become more expected and anticipated, listeners may grow less tolerant of off-key singers and more accepting of the "manufactured" sound that Auto-tune can produce.

Another factor related to personal preference is that not every voice is suited to digital manipulation. Think of Nina Simone, Bob Dylan, Neil Young, P.J. Harvey, and others with interesting and distinctive voices. Their singing would not be improved by Auto-tune. John Parish, a music producer who often works with those he calls "character" singers, says that Auto-tuning such performers would be like asking Jackson Pollock to stay within the lines.[11] We would diminish some of what makes them distinctive and interesting. But again, a preference for these types of voices is a personal inclination that is not necessarily shared by others. The fact that Bob Dylan would no longer sound like himself if Auto-tuned does not take away from the fact that Kesha or Selena Gomez or others may sound better if Auto-tuned, or that fans of these singers may have come to prefer Auto-tuned vocals.

There are indications that even Hildebrand has misgivings about some uses of the technology he invented. When Anderson interviewed him, he no longer compared Auto-tune to make-up. Instead he said, "I just make the car. I don't drive it down the wrong side of the road."[12] In other words, Auto-tune is a neutral technology (like the automobile) that may be misused, rather than something bad in itself or something (arguably) beneficial, like make-up.

Are Hildebrand and the proponents of Auto-tune correct? Is it a benign, money and time saving technology that is simply sometimes misused? Or do Auto-tune's detractors have a point and is any use of Auto-tune deceptive and therefore not benign? One argument sometimes put forward against Auto-tune (whether or not it is presented as an argument) is the position that vocals altered in this way sound unpleasant. Yet this view presents no more than a personal preference and is not particularly compelling. It would seem that some people like the effect of Auto-tune more than others and there is not much more to be said about it.

However, detractors of Auto-tune have at least one argument against it that is not easily dismissed. That is the expressive potential that is lost through the use of Auto-tune. The human voice is an analog instrument, capable of great nuances of pitch. In this way it resembles stringed instruments, which can be made to produce sounds at any point along their strings. The voice is not a digital instrument, still less is it an even-tempered instrument like the piano. Auto-tune, because it corrects pitches to the nearest semi-tone, effectively turns the voice into an even-tempered instrument. Yet intonation (whether a pitch is exact or not) conveys musical expression. This is true both for the voice and for any musical instrument that (unlike the piano) allows the performer to convey nuances of pitch. Singing (and music-making more generally) is not just about hitting the correct pitches. In some genres, "correct" (in the sense of even-tempered) intonation is not highly prized. In the words of Victor Coelho, a professor of music at the University of Boston, "When a (blues) singer is 'flat' it's not because he's doing it because he doesn't know any better. It's for inflection!"[13] While the variation of intonation for expressive purposes may be easiest to hear and most evident in blues, it is by no means unique to the blues or to blues-influenced genres. Even in classical (art) music, singers and instrumentalists may "slide" up to a notated pitch for expressive effect. (That is, they begin the note slightly flat.) And the technique of vibrato on string instruments, which can be used to enhance the expressivity of notes and phrases, is really a way of slightly varying pitch by moving the fingering hand back and forth quickly over a short distance.

The expressive potential of pitch is lost with the use of Auto-tune. This, to my mind, is its greatest aesthetic deficiency and it overtakes concerns about authenticity and about misrepresentation. Problems with Auto-tune do not dissolve even if everyone were to be honest and forthcoming about their use of it, and even if "community standards" find its use innocuous.

"Believe"

When Cher was preparing to work on her twenty-second studio album, Rob Dickins, the President of Warner Music U.K. told her that he wanted her to do a dance album.[14] Her previous album, a collection of rock ballads, had sold poorly. Cher wasn't thrilled by the idea. In her view, dance music was not "a genre with real songs." Dickins was determined to prove her wrong. He happened to run into songwriter Brian Higgins, who passed him a tape of 16 possible songs for the Cher album. Dickins was immediately taken with the half-finished "Believe." The chorus was solid, but the verses needed work, so Dickins brought in some staff songwriters. Eventually, there would be six songwriters credited on the song, with uncredited contributions by others.

When it came time to record and produce "Believe," other problems arose. No matter what they did, the verses sounded "lifeless." To take a break and get their minds off "Believe," Cher proposed they listen to a CD by Andrew Roachford she had recently bought. One of the songs used a vocorder to give the vocals a processed, robotic effect. Cher suggested they try something similar, the producers cranked up the settings on Auto-tune, Cher loved the effect, and the rest is popular music history.

I can't remember my first impression of "Believe," except that it was ubiquitous and I soon tired of it. The effect created by the use of Auto-tune on Cher's voice is now so common in popular and dance music that I can't recapture my first impressions of it. Listening to the song now (and watching the original video), I find that I like it more than I remembered.[15]

No one involved with the song denied that Cher's voice had been doctored although at first they were cagey about the origin of the effect. What questions can we ask about her recording, with respect to authenticity? Trivially, it is definitely and authentically Cher who is singing. She has a distinctive voice that is easy to recognize, even when processed. What of authenticity in the sense of sincerity? Cher is nothing if not a professional, and she definitely makes me feel that she "believes" in the song (pun not intended). A *New York Times* article about the origin of the song and recording also makes it clear that Cher wanted to make sure that she could sing the song in an authentic way. She told the interviewer that she was dissatisfied with the second verse as originally written, as it simply reiterated the "so sad that you're leaving" sentiment of the first verse. She said that she thought to herself, "You can be sad for one verse, but you can't be sad for two," and she came up with the lines, "I've had time to see it through/ Maybe I'm too good for you," instead.

Still, while Cher certainly sings the song with conviction, and even modified the lyrics to make sure that she could sing it with conviction, she doesn't (to my ears) sound particularly expressive. But perhaps asking for emotional expression in dance music is misguided, like expecting a danceable beat in lieder. After a little internet searching I found two additional versions of "Believe," neither of which contain obviously doctored vocals, and both versions sound more expressive than Cher's. I particularly liked the first, by British singer Hannah Trigwell, who accompanies herself on an acoustic guitar.[16] I find that Trigwell hits exactly the right balance for the song. She sounds sad, but not overwrought. Too much passion weighs the song down, which is the problem I have with the version by Cami Bradley.[17] And while both singers sound emotionally invested in the song, I cannot help but feel a little suspicious of Bradley. Does she really mean it or is she putting me on? Both Trigwell and Bradley, in their covers, take "Believe" out of the dance music genre and into a confessional "singer/songwriter" mode. In this type of music, obviously doctored vocals would be out of place. And while I feel that I can fairly compare Trigwell to Bradley, I don't feel like it would be proper to compare either to Cher. Cher's version is in a different genre and different standards are applicable.

Notes

1 Godlovitch, *Musical Performance*, 76–78.
2 Geoff Boucher, "Beat at Their Own Game," in Mickey Hart and Paul Bresnick (eds), *Da Capo Best Music Writing 2004* (Cambridge, MA: Da Capo Press, 2004), 27–33.
3 http://therangeplace.forummotions.com/t1136-billie-holiday?highlight=billie +holiday (accessed December 9, 2014).
4 http://therangeplace.forummotions.com/t2007-karen-carpenter?highlight=karen+car penter (accessed December 9, 2014).
5 http://youtu.be/wdWG2wgkfYs
6 http://operachic.typepad.com/opera_chic/2010/03/keeping-it-unreal-at-teatro-real-mic rophone-controversy-ignites-the-crowds.html
7 Lessley Anderson, "Seduced by 'Perfect Pitch': How Auto-Tune Conquered Popular Music," *The Verge*, February 27, 2013, www.theverge.com/2013/2/27/3964406/ seduced-by-perfect-pitch-how-auto-tune-conquered-pop-music (accessed December 9, 2014).
8 Brad Wheeler, "Michael Bublé and How Auto-Tune Became the Botox of Popular Music," *The Globe and Mail*, April 22, 2013, www.theglobeandmail.com/arts/

music/michael-buble-and-how-auto-tune-became-the-botox-of-pop-music/article1 1420371/ (accessed December 9, 2014).

9 Mike Hess, "Milli Vanilli, the Real Story – 20 Years Later," *Pop Eater*, January 29, 2010, www.popeater.com/2010/01/29/milli-vanilli-fab-morvan-grammy/ (accessed May 28, 2014).

10 Anderson, "Seduced by 'Perfect Pitch'."

11 Anderson, "Seduced by 'Perfect Pitch'."

12 Anderson, "Seduced by 'Perfect Pitch'."

13 Anderson, "Seduced by 'Perfect Pitch'."

14 Information about the song's history is taken from Neil Strauss, "Cher Resurrected, Again, by a Hit; The Long, Hard but Serendipitous Road to 'Believe'," *The New York Times*, March 11, 1989, www.nytimes.com/1999/03/11/arts/cher-resurrected-again-by-a-hit-the-long-hard-but-serendipitous-road-to-believe.html?src=pm&pagewanted=1 (accessed December 9, 2014).

15 http://youtu.be/4p0chD8U8fA

16 http://youtu.be/f8Dyfg3CjDw

17 http://youtu.be/-2QU7IiW17A

7   Performance
Ethical Considerations

Singers who perform in public have a variety of obligations. They have obligations to composers and lyricists; to musical and performance traditions; to their fellow musicians; and to audiences. Some of these obligations – to show up on time prepared to perform – are professional; many others are aesthetic. What of singers' ethical obligations? There is a small philosophical literature on the ethical obligations of musicians, but the focus has been on musicians' obligations to composers, and singing has not been paid special attention. In this chapter my main concern will be with singers' ethical obligations to their audiences. I will argue that in some cases singers have duties to audiences, both in their choice of material and in the details of their performance. First, I'll speak generally and in outline about singers' ethical obligations to their audiences. Then I'll draw out some implications for my position (including implications for those whose only singing is in the shower). I'll illustrate and test these claims through consideration of the American folksong "John Henry."

Singers' Ethical Obligations to Audiences

Who is a singer's audience? Most obviously, the audience consists of those in attendance at a live performance. Yet singers' obligations extend beyond an initial live audience of a specific performance and includes those future listeners who may hear the performance in a recording. In some instances, the audience to which a singer has obligations encompasses those for whom the song has a cultural or communal significance, whether or not they are in the present audience. An inappropriate performance of such a song can offend, and it can offend those who are not in the original audience. This is comparable to the way that a racist joke may offend those who are the butt of the joke, even if they are not present when it is told. (I realize that I have not yet explained what an "inappropriate" performance might be. That's coming.)

The potential for offense is easiest to see if we consider that much-derided category of songs, national anthems. As I suggested in Chapter 3, national anthems are songs intended for "participation-performance" or communal singing. When a solo vocalist sings the national anthem, he does so less for an audience than on behalf of an audience. The special standing of national anthems and their shared significance makes poor performances of them problematic for reasons that go beyond aesthetics. A poor public performance of a national anthem does not offend merely for aesthetic reasons, and does not offend merely those in the singer's initial audience. It may rightly offend those in the national group who receive a report of the poor performance, whether or not they ever hear it for themselves. (In the same way, the report that a racist joke has been told may offend those who have not heard the specifics of the joke.)

Let me return briefly to Beyoncé's use of a pre-recorded track while she sang the U.S. national anthem at President Obama's 2012 inauguration. This was controversial, not only because it made some detractors wonder if she could really sing. Even some of those who did not doubt her abilities thought that it was improper to perform the national anthem with technological help. The U.S. national anthem is traditionally performed live. To perform it with a "safety net" is to risk treating it as just another work for performance, rather than a work for participation-performance that "honors America" (as the sports announcers like to say). Beyoncé may have offended some because it seemed as though she was performing for them, rather than on their behalf.

The special status of national anthems is part of what accounts for the aesthetic power that intentionally disrespectful or irreverent performances can have. I am thinking here of the Sex Pistols' "God Save the Queen" and Jimi Hendrix's performance of "The Star Spangled Banner" at Woodstock. (To be exact, the Sex Pistols did not sing the standard lyrics or melody to "God Save the Queen" but even the use of the title and some of the lyrics was provocative. And Hendrix did not sing the U.S. national anthem but played it on guitar.) Calculatedly disrespectful renditions of national anthems are transgressive. Such overstepping of boundaries can be a source of aesthetic power and value, the desire to "épater les bourgeois," being a running motif in art since at least the Romantic era.

National anthems, like other symbols of the state, have a special legal status. But other songs may be similarly meaningful to, and significant for, racial, cultural or national groups, without having such official status. These songs, and the concerns they raise, have been largely overlooked by philosophers (especially analytic philosophers) who have tended to concentrate on art music and to treat art as divorced from social and political factors. I have in mind songs like "Gens du pays," which has been called the unofficial national anthem of the Quebecois; hymns and Christmas carols, with their special resonance for Christians; Americans may have a special connection to songs such as "Georgia on my Mind," "The Yellow Rose of Texas," "My Old Kentucky Home," and "Shenandoah"; for the Irish, a song called "The Foggy Dew" set to the tune of the traditional English ballad commemorates the Easter Uprising of 1916; and certain spirituals including "We Shall

Overcome" and "Go Down Moses" became important to those in the 1960s' civil rights movement.

Some of the songs I just listed are traditional or folk songs. The categories "folk music" and more generally "folk art" are highly contested. Attempts to define them tend to show up the limits of our categories rather than to be genuinely informative. However, there is one quality of the folksong, as traditionally defined, that is relevant here: folk songs are ontologically thin. We have seen that their lyrics are malleable – verses may be sung out of order or dropped; melodies and rhythms may vary from one region to the next, or even from one singer to the next. Instrumentation is also flexible – the song may be sung a cappella or with whatever accompaniment is available. Consequently folk musicians generally have much more freedom and flexibility in their performance practices than do musicians who engage with art music. Whatever freedom singers have in their performances comes with a responsibility. For the rest of this chapter, I will focus on genres in which the singer has, relatively speaking, a wide scope of choice in performance. The ethical issues in singing performance are easiest to see here.

In its broadest and one of its more ancient understandings, "ethics" is the search for the best way to live. Today its significance is often taken to be a good deal more narrow, not to say legalistic. When I talk about the "ethics of singing" I mean "ethics" to be taken in a very broad sense. The choices singers make rarely extend to the morally right or wrong, still less often to good versus evil. I assume that singers, generally, do not seek to offend or disrespect their listeners. I set aside those cases where it is clear that, for aesthetic or political reasons, disrespect is exactly what is intended. The kind of moral violations that singers can make are more commonly violations of moral sensitivity. But what may begin as a sin of omission, if discovered and left uncorrected, becomes something else: a tangible moral failing, not to say a flaw of character. My main claim in this chapter is that to perform a song in a morally sensitive manner requires moral deference. When a song is valued by a group, whether for musical or for extra-musical reasons, a morally sensitive singer must try to understand why the song has the significance that it does, and must shape the details of her performance so as to respect or honor that significance. If she does not, then she risks giving offense.

I borrow the notion of "moral deference" from philosopher Laurence Thomas.[1] The idea behind moral deference is both simple and reasonable: the morally significant experiences of others will sometimes be opaque to us. There is no perspective from which any and every person will always be able to grasp the experiences of another. Even with sincerity and good will, we must not assume that we are always fully capable of grasping another's experiences – the challenges, pain, and anxiety that he or she has undergone or continues to experience. To believe otherwise, to assume that such understanding can always be achieved, is to be guilty of moral hubris. Thomas offers two reasons why our capacity for imaginative reconstruction of another's experiences is limited. First, we can never be the subject of another's experience as even a complete description cannot convey the subjective element of an experience. Second, we do not live with the memories of another's experience, and these memories do not continue to shape our lives.

Moral deference is the appropriate attitude to take when trying to understand others who have been subject to social injustice. Although anyone can suffer a misfortune, and any misfortune can challenge our capacities for imaginative understanding, some misfortunes are tied to membership of what Thomas calls "diminished social categories." Members of diminished social categories are constituted by others not to see themselves as full and equal members of society. Such constitution can be explicit – think of the heckler who told Hillary Clinton to "iron my shirts" while she was campaigning for the Democratic presidential nomination. Or it can be subtle – one example is what former U.S. president George W. Bush called the "soft bigotry of lowered expectations" in grade-school classrooms that shape a child's view of himself and his place in the world.[2] The misfortunes tied to membership of a diminished social category are particularly difficult for people not in such categories to understand, and moral deference is thus more acutely required with respect to them.

What is it to behave with moral deference, to adopt it as an attitude? While the rationale for moral deference may be easy to grasp, its actual tangible constraints and obligations are not. Thomas is disappointingly brief in his discussion of what, specifically, moral deference requires of us. Very suggestively for my purposes, Thomas invokes the notion of "bearing witness." Moral deference is to be made concrete by thinking of what it means to bear witness to another's moral pain with her authorization. This requires that one has gained the trust and confidence of another to speak in an informed manner and with conviction on her behalf about the moral pain she has endured. One will be able to convey what was salient for another in the way that it was salient for her. Crucially, one will refrain from using another's moral pain as a means to convey *one's own* moral perspective or pain. To be able to bear witness to another's pain effectively and with conviction requires a preliminary stage, and this stage is at the heart of what it means to practice moral deference. It is to earn the trust of another and listen to her story, picking up on emotional nuances and non-verbal behavior, and through such active listening to have insight into how another's life has been emotionally configured by these experiences.

Before continuing, I want to address a worry about my use of the concept of moral deference. Is everyone obliged to adopt an attitude of moral deference? To practice moral deference is to acquire a new set of sensibilities about what it is to live as an oppressed person in an unjust society. Like any new sensitivity, it comes with increased vulnerability, in this case vulnerabilities to the pain caused by social injustice. Thomas warns that it is "not an activity for the faint of heart."[3] So it would seem that, because of the great demands it makes on us, moral deference cannot be a general social obligation. At the same time Thomas also insists that a studied refusal to engage in the moral learning at the heart of moral deference is a manifestation of oppression and even "adds insult to injury."[4] I suggest that moral deference is best seen as akin to a Kantian imperfect duty. According to Kant, we have a duty to help others, but because we cannot possibly help everyone who might require it, this duty is imperfect only. So while we have a perfect (that is, without exception) duty never to treat another person merely as a means, our duty to help others does in fact admit of exceptions. We are not obliged to help everyone who asks it of us.[5] Similarly, we might have an imperfect duty to develop some moral sensitivities, including the attitude of moral deference. As a matter of practical fact, given constraints of time and psychological stress, it would be impossible to develop moral sensitivity to every individual and group who deserves it. Yet it is incumbent upon us to develop moral sensitivities to some individuals and groups, inasmuch as we desire to be treated with moral sensitivity ourselves.[6]

"John Henry"

To understand how singers can exhibit moral deference we need to consider a specific song. I have chosen "John Henry" both because of its enduring popularity, and because of the hold that the character John Henry continues to have on the American popular imagination. Elements of the song can be traced to the British ballad tradition (Welshmen mined coal in the mountains near where John Henry worked), to the African-American convicts and laborers who used the song to regulate their work, to blues musicians such as W.C. Handy who published the first sheet music for the song, and to the musicians involved in the 1960s' folk music revival.

"John Henry" has been called the most frequently recorded American folksong, and it is estimated that nearly 100 new versions have been recorded since the mid-1990s alone.[7] The song straddles a number of traditions, being both one of the first songs to be called "the blues" and one of the first recorded country songs. Renditions have been recorded by Leadbelly, Paul Robeson, Woody Guthrie, Pete Seeger, Johnny Cash, Van Morrison, and Bruce Springsteen, among others. Alt-country musicians Gillian Welch, Joe Uehlein and the U-Liners, and the Drive-By Truckers have also recently recorded the folksong or written an original song based on the legend of John Henry. Librarians at the Library of Congress estimate that John Henry is the most intensively researched character in American folklore.[8] In addition to the song, he has been the inspiration for statues, novels, posters, paintings, films, stage dramas, academic studies, and a parody in *The Onion* satirical newspaper.[9]

When a figure has been of enduring relevance to a wide variety of people, it seems safe to say that a number of factors contribute to his status. Certainly, John Henry has meant many things to many people (although I would resist the implication that John Henry is a cipher or that he can mean anything to anyone). Various versions of the song place his origin in different U.S. states and even in the British Isles. Although no version of the song that I have come across mentions his racial identity, he is widely understood to be African-American. John Henry is a symbol of physical strength and endurance; of exploited labor; of the dignity of a human being against the degradations of the machine age; and of racial pride and solidarity. During WWII his image was used in U.S. government propaganda as a symbol of social tolerance and diversity.

While the song reflects historical events, there is much controversy among historians and folklorists about who exactly John Henry was, where he lived, on which rail lines he worked, and why he died. Although he worked for a railway and has often been pictured driving rail spikes into ties, his work was actually more like that of a miner. He was probably a member of a crew doing the difficult and dangerous job of blasting through mountains, hammering holes where dynamite charges could be laid. The earliest versions of the song are slow and rather stately hammer songs. A "hammer song" is a type of work song used by both miners and railway trackliners to regulate the timing of their hammer blows. These songs are slow because working too quickly would lead both to exhaustion and to a lack of precision in the hammer blows, putting the shaker – the worker who held the chisel or drill – at risk. In these songs, death and escape are frequent themes.

To my mind, the theme of work, and in particular of the dignity of physical work, is absolutely crucial to John Henry's legend, to his enduring appeal, and to the folksong itself. John Henry is defined by the work he does; he is, primarily, the "steel driving man." The song's lyrics stress his great strength and physical courage. The miners and railway men who first sang the song, taught it to their co-workers, and carried it with them to new job sites, found in John Henry's exploits a reflection of their own values and ideals. Much like blue collar workers today, they saw hard work as conferring dignity and marking a moral boundary between themselves and others.[10] Note these prominent lyrics, found in every version of the song I know of. When John Henry's captain tells him about the steam drill, he replies:

A man ain't nothing but a man
But before I let that steel beat me down
I will die with this hammer in my hand[11]

The theme of the dignity of work is also indicated in a curious verse shared by many versions of the song. When John Henry is too sick to work, or in some versions after his death, it is said:

Well they called John Henry's woman
Yes they called for Julie-Anne

Well she picked up the hammer where John Henry lay
And she drove that steel like a man, Great God!
And she drove that steel just like a man

Here, working and driving steel "like a man" is clearly meant as commendatory; there is no disapproval indicated at the subversion of gender roles. John Henry's legacy is that he inspires and enables others to work. One historian has speculated that this passage refers to the "race work" that women had to do in the absence of male members of the community, who died young or were jailed in disproportionate numbers by the racially biased laws of the Reconstruction period.[12] (The same historian believes that the historical John Henry was himself a victim of such laws.) Whether Julie-Anne does the literal work of driving steel or this passage is best interpreted as a metaphor, her work helps support the community and is valued by it.

If I am correct, and the dignity of work is at least an important aspect of what has made the character of John Henry and songs celebrating him of such enduring relevance, then how should such considerations affect a singer's performance? How can a singer who has taken on the requisite moral deference to understand the reasons for the song's importance make his understanding clear in his performance? I would say that such understanding is manifest in the singer's choices regarding which version of the song to sing, which verses are sung and which are omitted, which verses begin and end the song, the accompanying instrumentation, and overall attitude. This last aspect, the attitude to the song conveyed in performance, is particularly important as it is by this means that a singer expresses his thoughts and feelings about the material sung – whether he adopts an attitude of irony or sincerity, for example.

Turning now to specific recordings of "John Henry," we can discern at least two broad approaches to the song's performance. The first is shared by Leadbelly, Pete Seeger, and Bruce Springsteen.[13] In this approach, the song "rocks out." The tempo is relatively fast. The performers, we can often sense, are having a great time. In Seeger's live version the audience even sings along. While all of these performers fulfill their aesthetic obligations as performers, it is not clear that they do justice to their ethical obligations. I can best illustrate this by a contrast with the second approach, one taken by Paul Robeson and by Valentine Pringle on Henry Belafonte's *The Long Road to Freedom: An Anthology of Black Music*. In this approach, the tempo is slower and the emphasis is on the song's lyrics rather than rhythm or melody. The song is explicitly and self-consciously *performed* for us. In the case of Pringle's performance on the Belafonte anthology, the musical arrangement is explicitly stylized. There is no attempt to recapture how the song might have sounded when sung by miners or trackliners. The musicians have explicitly rejected the notion of "authenticity" as recapturing a purported past. Instead they try to convey the ideal of how the song might sound in an exemplary performance.[14]

The approach to the song taken by Pringle and Belafonte on *The Long Road to Freedom* contrasts sharply with the approach taken by Springsteen on his self-produced album, *We Shall Overcome: The Seeger Sessions*. Springsteen, in his liner notes, stresses the un-stylized, "authentic" character of the performances. He tells us that he had only recently met most of the musicians he plays with and had not played with them until the day they started recording, in the living room of his house. He continues:

> This is a LIVE recording, everything cut in three one-day sessions ('97, '05, '06) with no rehearsals. All arrangements were conducted as we played, you can hear me shouting out the names and instruments of the players as we roll. This approach takes the listener along for the whole ride, as you hear the music not just being played but being *made*. So, turn it up, put on your dancin' and singin' shoes, and have fun. We did.[15]

Sophisticated listeners will take Springsteen's characterization of the project with good humor, but hopefully also with some skepticism. The musicians he performs with on the album are seasoned professionals; whether or not they had seen the arrangements or rehearsed together beforehand is really beside the point. The enjoyment they derive from playing together does not diminish their musical accomplishment or their professional status. The performance captured over those three days and offered to us is no less a *performance*, while also being a documentary of a bunch of people having fun. I suspect that Springsteen stresses the unrehearsed, spontaneous, and joyful character of his project out of an attachment to an ideal of rock-and-roll authenticity as sincerity. But whatever is gained for authenticity here is lost ground elsewhere. People who sound like they are having fun are hardly the best suited to be telling a story of a man driven to his death by overwork, whatever hope or resilience we also take from the story.

Pringle's version is different in a number of additional ways from Springsteen's and from the other versions under discussion. It begins with this verse sung by a male chorus:[16]

> Well every Monday morning
> When the bluebirds begin to sing
> You can hear those hammers for a mile or more
> Oh you can hear John Henry's hammer ring, Lord
> You can hear John Henry's hammer ring

While other performances include this verse, few begin with it. The verse is in the present tense; the implication is that you can *still* hear John Henry's hammer. He wasn't killed in the contest with the steam drill, after all. Another distinctive element of Pringle's performance is that the musical accompaniment mimics and so recalls the hammer blows in earlier work-song versions of the song. Pringle's attitude to the material is reverent. He does not particularly sound like he is having a good time; rather, he sounds like he is telling us something important, something that he wants us to hear. And he sounds like he is moved by what he is telling us. I also find it significant that Pringle ends with this verse:

> Oh they took John Henry to the graveyard
> And they buried him in the sand
> And every locomotive come rolling by
> Said, "There lies a steel driving man, Lord.
> John Henry was a steel driving man."

The effect is similar to that of the first verse. We know that John Henry has not been forgotten. He, and the example he set, live in the memory.

A few clarifications before continuing: first, just as there is more than one way to perform a song well, there is more than one way to perform a song with moral deference, and indeed more than one way to practice moral deference more generally. I do not believe that every morally appropriate performance of "John Henry" will sound like every other or that each will share features with the performances I have discussed here. There may be ways to sing "John Henry" with moral deference that I have not imagined. Second, a singer whose performance seems to express moral deference has not necessarily adopted it as an attitude. In this case there are no necessary and direct links from performance to character. He or she may be singing the song in a certain way for purely aesthetic reasons. Such a situation is analogous to that of a non-Russian-speaking baritone who has learned his part in *Boris Gudunov* phonetically, but does not understand the literal meaning of the syllables he sings. There are similarly no necessary and direct links from character to performance. A singer may have a genuine attitude of moral deference to a song, yet lack the skills to convey that attitude in performance.

Moral Deference and Singing Performance

Memory is at the heart of Thomas' notion of moral deference. The persistence of memory is both what makes moral deference necessary and what makes it possible. The memory of past injustice shapes an individual's responses in the present. Adopting an attitude of moral deference means recognizing that the memories and experiences of others are always, in an important sense, opaque to us. Since a community's memories are so often captured and transmitted through its music, it seems especially appropriate to practice moral deference with regard to that music. We'll see that this position has implications beyond the ones already indicated for singers.

The position I have outlined in this chapter has implications for the discussions of authenticity in the previous chapter and to more broadly construed questions of cultural appropriation. Joel Rudinow's argument, that authenticity can be secured through proximity to a tradition, is most useful in cases where the tradition itself is relatively delimited and of living memory. In the case of the song "John Henry," the tradition is sufficiently broad and varied that every singer I have mentioned can claim to be an heir and to have proximity to it. What of songs that are part of a such a broad and inclusive tradition, but have special significance for a smaller group? It would seem then that the need for moral deference and for "bearing witness" with sensitivity is all the more pressing.

In the previous chapter I expressed some skepticism about the importance of authenticity to the philosophy of music (as opposed to its importance to fans). If I am correct about the ethical aspect of singing, then whether or not a singer shows appropriate moral deference should be evident to anyone who has familiarized herself with the material in question, knows something of its possible importance to an audience, and listens attentively. Membership in a specific social group or fan base is neither necessary nor sufficient. This means that the notion of moral deference is more powerful and fruitful than the concept of authenticity for philosophers and other scholars interested in the intersections between art and social identity.

The importance of attentive listening brings me to another implication of my position. Here I shift from discussing singers to discussing their audiences. Philosophers, including Roger Scruton, Martha Nussbaum, Colin Radford, Matthew Kieran, and others, have tried to identify the links between moral and aesthetic sensitivity, between listening to the "right" music or reading the "right" books and having the "right" sort of character. I do not think that any of these attempts has been successful, and my position allows us to see why. It is not a matter of the "right" aesthetic sources, but listening and attending *in the right way*. Moral deference can be adopted by fans of any musical genre or form of aesthetic expression. It does not depend on cultivating one's tastes to appreciate "higher" art forms or genres. At the heart of moral deference is thinking about others – their struggles, their experience in an unjust society. Thinking about one's *own* aesthetic or moral sensitivity is fundamentally at odds with adopting an attitude of moral deference. This focus on the pain of others – both historically and currently – whether expressed through art or more plainly in the course of daily life, is one way in which we can attend "in the right way." Moral sensitivity behooves those who listen to music as well as those who make it. Adopting an attitude of moral deference – finding out which songs might be important to which audiences, thinking about why certain material has the significance that it does, and what kind of performance best honors this significance – will increase our sensitivity as listeners. If we listen well enough it will also increase our moral sensitivity more generally, and such a result could only be to the good.

Notes

1 Laurence Thomas, "Moral Deference," *The Philosophical Forum* 24:1–3 (1992–93), 233–50.

2 Text of George W. Bush's Speech to the NAACP, July 10, 2000, www.washing tonpost.com/wp-srv/onpolitics/elections/bushtext071000.htm (accessed January 12, 2008).

3 Thomas, "Moral Deference," 247.

4 Thomas, "Moral Deference," 247.

5 See Immanuel Kant, *Grounding for the Metaphysics of Morals*, trans. James W. Ellington (Indianapolis: Hackett, 2001), 31–33.

6 I do not know whether Thomas would develop his position in this way, and I do not claim that he would.

7 Scott Reynolds Nelson, *Steel Drivin' Man – John Henry – The Untold Story of an American Legend* (Oxford University Press, 2006), 172.

8 Nelson, *Steel Drivin' Man*, 2.

9 "Modern-Day John Henry Dies Trying to Out-Spreadsheet Excel 11.0," *The Onion*, February 27, 2006, www.theonion.com/content/news/modern_day_john_henry_ dies_trying (accessed December 20, 2007).

10 See Michèle Lamont, *The Dignity of Working Men: Morality and the Boundaries of Race, Class, and Immigration* (Cambridge, MA: Harvard University Press, 2000).

11 All of the lyrics in this paper have been transcribed from the version sung by Valentine Pringle on *Long Road to Freedom: An Anthology of Black Music* (2001).

12 Nelson, *Steel Drivin' Man*, 107.

13 Leadbelly, Volume 7 (1947–49); Bruce Springsteen, *We Shall Overcome: The Seeger Sessions* (2006).

14 Michael Eldridge, "Remains of the Day-O: A Conversation with Harry Belafonte," in Mickey Hart and Paul Bresnick (eds), *Da Capo Best Music Writing 2004* (Cambridge, MA: Da Capo Press, 2004), 68–92.

15 *We Shall Overcome: The Seeger Sessions*. Liner notes by Bruce Springsteen.

16 *Long Road to Freedom: An Anthology of Black Music*, Volume 4.

8   Song and Drama

Tolstoy Visits the Opera

In the opening pages of his treatise *What is Art?* Leo Tolstoy describes a visit he once made to the rehearsal of a new opera production. He was not, to say the least, favorably impressed.

As he walked through the cavernous backstage area past immense stage machinery, Tolstoy noticed a workman, "pale, haggard, in a dirty blouse, with dirty, work-worn hands and cramped fingers" angrily berating another. Making his way closer to the stage, he saw "dozens, if not hundreds" of dancers and chorus members – men "in costumes fitting tight to their thighs and calves" and women "as nearly nude as might be." He noted the presence of three directors – a conductor, a theatre director, and a dancing-master – "whose salary per month exceeded what ten laborers earn in a year." Moving from the backstage to the house, Tolstoy watched seemingly endless repetitions of the scene being rehearsed. The action was stopped again and again: either the chorus had not entered in a satisfactory manner, or a musician had played a wrong note (and was publicly humiliated by the conductor), or the singers had to be corrected. The plot – something about an Indian king who disguises himself in order to meet incognito the woman to whom he has been betrothed – seemed utterly preposterous. The rehearsal lasted six hours; the scene under rehearsal was repeated about twenty times; the conductor acted like a petty tyrant; and the musicians and singers seemed completely demoralized. Tolstoy's overall assessment? "It would be difficult to find a more repulsive sight."[1]

Now, Tolstoy did not lead a sheltered life. By 1897, when *What is Art?* was published, he had witnessed terrible poverty as a census taker in some of the most squalid parts of Moscow, had fought in the Crimean War, and had been excommunicated by the Russian Orthodox church. Yet he singled out an opera rehearsal for this extraordinary condemnation.

Tolstoy found several things to dislike about opera. The puritan in him objected to the revealing costumes and to the amounts of money spent on unnecessary luxury. His humanitarian nature disapproved of the hostility that the production seemed to have brought out in everyone from simple workmen to the conductor. But I think that the biggest reason for Tolstoy's visceral response can be traced to his philosophy of art. Tolstoy believed that sincerity was the most important gauge of art's value. He argued that art is a kind of language, but a language used to convey emotion rather than thought. Good art, he believed, is "infectious" – it is capable of conveying clear and deep emotion to a large number of people. So the best art is accessible rather than difficult. And while art conveys emotion, not all emotions are equal. The best art conveys morally superior emotions; that is, emotions that aid in communal life. An artist can create this kind of work and "infect" a great number of people only if he or she is sincere. Tolstoy was never one to shrink from the implications of his ideas, and so he rejected several works usually considered to be art, if not great art: Beethoven's Ninth Symphony (which he doubted could be widely understood or enjoyed); Shakespeare's plays (which he thought rarely sent the correct moral message); and indeed his own earlier novels.

With this (brief) summary of Tolstoy's theory of art it is easier to see why opera upset him so much. He doubted that such a spectacle could appeal to the vast majority of ordinary people. It seemed distinctly aimed at the pampered and decadent upper classes. And even if opera could somehow be made more accessible, it fails to communicate morally superior emotions. We know this because so many of the participants Tolstoy observed seem morally stunted – angry and tyrannical for no good reason, or craven in the face of ill treatment. Tolstoy began his book with opera so as to set up an example of the kind of art he meant to reject. Opera is, for him, the epitome of insincere or artificial art: unrealistic plots with characters unlike any real human beings, conveyed by stylized singing and histrionic action to the accompaniment of complicated orchestral music. As he wrote, "If there are, occasionally, good melodies in the opera to which it is pleasant to listen, they could have been sung simply, without these stupid costumes and all the processions and recitatives and hand-wavings."[2]

We need not accept Tolstoy's philosophy of art nor his assessment of opera. Opera is a highly conventional art form. These conventions – that characters sing rather than speak, that music is heard throughout, that plots may be contrived, that performers need not resemble the characters they play – are part of what makes opera so appealing for some and so alienating to others. I find it interesting that some of the people today who profess to dislike opera do so for reasons similar to those given by Tolstoy. They find it, well, too theatrical, too artificial. After all, who really expresses their thoughts and feelings in song? And even those who enjoy (non-operatic) musical theatre and movie musicals (and are thereby accepting of theatricality) find other things to object about in opera: why does the action have to come to a halt so often? The funny thing is that those who love opera do so for some of the same reasons: the extreme theatricality and the heightened emotion that can be conveyed through music and singing as opposed to straight speech.

This chapter is on song and drama rather than about opera specifically. Opera is particularly interesting because it can be seen as the "extreme" form of musical drama, and so the problems of song and drama come out most sharply here. I see the different art forms involving song and drama as forming a continuum. At one end (let's call it the non-operatic pole) are dramatic productions (and by this I mean to include stage plays, filmed plays and movies) that happen to include singing. Farther along the continuum are "musicals" – dramatic productions in which singing is conceived of as an important aspect and one that audiences especially prize. Even farther along are musicals that are "sung through"; that is, the singing is more-or-less continuous and there is little or no spoken dialogue. Examples include *Rent*, *Cats*, *Evita*, and *The Phantom of the Opera*.

Since operas and non-operatic musicals alike may be sung through, do we need to preserve a distinction between them? Would it not be better to employ Occam's Razor and discuss them together? I argue that we should preserve the distinction, even though there will always be tricky borderline cases and composers who want to blur the distinctions. The critic Anthony Tommasini argues that the main difference between opera and musicals is that in musicals, words have the upper edge, and in opera, the music does. From this basic difference, he says, other defining aspects follow, including singing style, orchestration, the importance of melody, and musical complexity.[3] I would go a little further. Virtuosic vocal display is part of the substance of opera – one of the things that goes to making opera what it is, and one of the things that fans prize. While non-operatic musicals may also sometimes include instances of virtuosic vocal display, they are not one of its defining features and not what adherents of the genre typically value. While the same people may attend both opera and musicals (and concerts and theatre productions), I suspect that they go to these different productions with different expectations. I am in agreement here with philosopher Bernard Williams who wrote that in opera, "a concrete feeling of performance and of the performers' artistry is nearer the front of the mind than in other dramatic arts."[4]

How Not to Think about Music Drama

My focus in this chapter is on songs within music dramas, but before going further I need to say something more about the nature of music drama itself. (Again, I'll stick with opera here because, as the most "extreme" form of music drama, the issues are easiest to see.) What sort of a thing is a music drama? I cannot offer the kind of definition that many philosophers would demand – one with necessary and sufficient conditions, meant to cover all possible instances, and which is typically defended through a process of explaining away counter-examples. Yet I do want to rule out two ways of approaching music drama that strike me as unpromising.

The first approach I mean to reject treats music dramas as long songs. An uncharitable reading of Levinson might imply that he takes such an approach. In his "Song and Music Drama"[5] he treats operas as, in effect, long songs, with the problem of "fit" between musical and non-musical elements being the same in both, although more difficult in musical drama. Robert Yanal is more explicit on this point. For him, "operatic drama" includes grand opera, oratorio, cantata, readings with music, and simple songs. Indeed, he says, "song is minimal opera."[6]

Yanal's approach ignores a distinction I discussed earlier, between songs that are "works for performance" and those that are not. Instead he lumps all different kinds of songs together and in effect treats all songs as works for performance. Even if we limit the discussion to songs that are works for performance, Yanal's move to treat all such vocal music in the same way is problematic in that it ignores the distinction between simple performance and dramatic performance. A singer in a music drama is playing a character; he or she does not sing *in propria persona*. Other singers also perform, of course, but in most cases they are better understood as performing themselves or performing exaggerated or caricatured versions of themselves, rather than as performing dramatic characters. If we don't keep this difference in mind, we risk misunderstanding the nature of dramatic song and of vocal performance more generally.

Levinson and Yanal both accept the hybrid model of songs and opera, whereby the constitutive elements of both (words and music in the first case and music and theatre in the second) are still evident and should be taken into account in our responses. To be fair, if one accepts the hybrid model and the main problem one wants to address is the relationship between words and music, then it may not matter where one makes the divisions, so to speak. The same issues arise whether one examines a single aria or the opera of which it is a part. I have already explained in Chapter 2 why I believe that the hybrid model of song is mistaken, and why evaluating songs according to the "fit" between music and words is an inadequate approach.

The second way of thinking about music drama that I mean to reject treats it as a literary genre. Yanal writes that an operatic performance of a text interprets a "literary artwork" and later (indicating that this was not a slip of the pen), he says that operatic drama "presents *a literary world* by means of music, usually along with some theatrical devices."[7] Yanal sees the music in opera as in service to the libretto or text. For me, this gets opera exactly backwards. It seems more plausible that the libretto provides an occasion or excuse for the music. Some evidence: first, operas are identified with composers, not librettists. We talk about Mozart's *Don Giovanni*, not Da Ponte's. Indeed, Da Ponte is one of the few librettists whose name may be familiar to non-specialists. Second, audiences may not understand the language that the opera is sung in, and this does not seem a barrier to enjoyment. Is there any other "literary genre" of which this can be said? While the use of surtitles to facilitate comprehension of the text is now widespread, not everyone agrees that this adds to the experience of attending an opera, and some argue that it actually detracts from the experience.

Finally, while there are exceptions, opera plots tend to be the subject of derision. This doesn't seem to matter to many fans; they appreciate opera for the music, and the storylines are a secondary consideration.

Does this mean that the hybrid model has no place in discussions of music drama? Not necessarily. I believe that some musicals, particularly those that are not sung through, are best understood and evaluated as examples of a hybrid art form. The better the music, the less the story and the theatrical elements matter; if the story and spectacle are very engaging, we tend to be forgiving towards the music when evaluating the experience as a whole. (Indeed, if the story is engaging enough, some audience members may not notice the music very much at all.) But the hybrid model fits opera and sung-through musicals less well and these seem to me to merit a different approach (although I cannot offer a fully worked-out theory of music drama). Some of the same concerns that lead me to reject the hybrid model for songs come into play here. An interest in how the music "fits" the text becomes an exercise in literary criticism, not in music appreciation. It leads to a bias against music dramas where the text cannot stand alone, over-looking the fact that these texts were often not meant to stand alone. Like a good song, a good music drama is one that provides audiences with a good (rich, fulfilling) experience, rather than one that displays the "correct" relationship between words and music. And while a good libretto contributes to some of the operas that provide such an experience, a good libretto seems neither necessary nor sufficient to a good music drama.

The Ontology of Singing in Music Drama

Singing can serve a variety of functions within a single dramatic production. Singing can advance the plot, reveal character, contribute to character development, or show the relationship between characters. Singing can also provide an audience distraction from set changes, or it may serve no other purpose than to provide enjoyment to the audience. This variety of functions, and the different scenarios that can arise from them, means that the ontological status of singing can vary from drama to drama. Different functions also make different kinds of demands on performers and elicit different kinds of audience expectations. So it is worth exploring these various possibilities in some detail.

In some dramatic productions, singing happens as a natural part of the plot. Perhaps the characters are also singers, or perhaps they find themselves in a situation where it would be natural or habitual to sing in life (say, in church or around a campfire). Kivy, following Cone, calls such performances examples of "realistic song." These performances are diegetic; that is, they are understood as being heard by the other characters in the drama (unlike, say, the background soundtrack music that is a part of the audience's experience, but not the characters'). Examples include the movies in which Elvis Presley played a character who was also a singer (such as

Jailhouse Rock, King Creole, and *Loving You.*) This gave the film producers ample opportunity to showcase his singing as part of a film's plot. Or the many movies in which the characters (who may or may not be presented as professional singers) must – for one reason or another – put on a show which we later see. This trope dates to the earliest days of movie musicals and was rejuvenated by Disney's *High School Musical* franchise.

Cone distinguished between "realistic" song and "operatic (or conventional or expressive) song." In the latter, singing replaces what would in a more naturalistic medium be speech. These vocal performances may or may not be intended to be part of the world of the drama. When a character (not previously identified as a singer) alone on stage sings to the audience, the singing is likely to be conventional or expressive, rather than realistic. Cone made this distinction in the course of discussing opera, and Kivy has taken it up and applied it to film.[8] I think Kivy's move is a good one, as the problems that Cone identified in opera arise in other dramatic forms that include singing.

Like some operas, many stage plays and movies combine realistic and conventional singing performances. For example, the classic film *Meet Me in St. Louis* contains unambiguously realistic song performances when the Smith family gathers around the piano to listen to their mother and father sing a duet, and when Tootie (Margaret O'Brien) and Esther (Judy Garland) entertain party guests by singing a popular song of the day. And it contains at least one clear example of conventional singing, when Esther, alone in the darkened house, sings "The Boy Next Door." Other song performances contain elements of both and are not so easy to categorize. When Esther sings "Have Yourself a Merry Little Christmas" to her youngest sister, it is not clear to me whether Esther is "really" singing – as she might be since we know her as a character who is comfortable expressing herself through song – or whether her singing is more like a stand-in for speech.

Cone claims that the "fundamental operatic ambiguity" is whether the characters are meant to be understood as speaking or as singing. We've seen that the same ambiguity can be present in stage and movie musicals. It is fairly clear what is going on in realistic song performances, especially when there is an audience on the stage or on the screen to signal to the "at-home" or "in-theatre" audience what is going on. But what are characters doing when they sing without an on-stage audience or when they communicate with one another in song rather than speech? Do these characters know that they are singing?

Cone offers some intriguing possible answers. In *The Composer's Voice* (1974) he argued that the character or the vocal persona (whether in opera or art song performance) does not consciously know that he is singing or hearing musical accompaniment, but subconsciously he does. In a later article, "The World of Opera and Its Inhabitants," Cone defends the idea that operatic characters are singer-composers.[9] Kivy, in a friendly article, takes up and explores this suggestion. However, Kivy qualifies his remarks:

he does not mean that all operatic characters can be understood as composing the songs they sing, nor that he has proposed a "theory" of opera. Rather, he offers the reader an invitation: "An imaginative way of looking at our world, and at the world of opera, that makes some kind of sense out of the latter in relation to the former."[10] In response, David Rosen throws cold water on both Cone and Kivy. "Is it reasonable – or interesting –," he asks, "to seek in opera the degree of consistency we find in the real world, and then be perplexed when we do not find it?"[11]

As a philosopher, I find myself torn between (on the one hand) a "totalizing" impulse to come up with a coherent and well-worked-out theory to answer these questions once and for all and (on the other hand) Rosen's bracing anti-theoretical skepticism. It seems to me that Kivy and Rosen are actually not that far from one another, despite the different ways they express their positions. Both agree that there can be no one-size answer that will fit all operas. Yet while these are intriguing questions, for me they are less significant than the question of what all of this means for audiences. How do audiences interpret the activities of characters in music drama? How does this affect their aesthetic experience? And I think that the answers are, "it depends" and "surprisingly little."

I am reminded of a possibly apocryphal story about Michael Curtiz, the director of *Casablanca*, *Mildred Pierce*, *The Adventures of Robin Hood*, and over 100 other films. When the screenwriter Howard Koch complained to Curtiz that he was making a character act illogically, Curtiz would brush away his concerns with, "Who cares about character? I make it go so fast nobody knows."[12] While Curtiz was reassuring Koch about his skill as a film maker, his off-hand remark also makes an important general aesthetic claim. If an audience is involved in a drama, they will overlook or forgive lapses in logic and inconsistencies. I think the same holds true for music drama. If the audience is involved in a performance, they will not stop to think about whether a character is "really" singing or not.

That characters in music drama sing rather than speak (some of the time or all of the time), and that sometimes they sing when they are alone, and that somehow previously unrelated characters all know the words and music of the same song, are conventions. And audiences – even very young audience members – seem to have no trouble accepting these conventions and enjoying performances based on them. I think this is evident from the great financial success that stage musicals enjoy. While I don't think that the market is necessarily a good barometer of artistic excellence, the fact that so many people attend musicals indicates to me that they value and enjoy the experience. If ontological issues about singing were distracting, I doubt that musicals would be as popular as they are. Now, these conventions may have been alienating in the early days of the genre. Similarly, people who have not been acculturated so as to be familiar with these conventions and children watching their first musicals may find the ontological complications raised by realistic and expressive singing to be distracting. Perhaps those who dislike musicals also find the conventions hard to swallow. But none of this detracts from my claim that, at least for those audience members who are familiar with and enjoy musicals, the conventions of the genre do not present obstacles to appreciation. (Frankly, I find the conventions of the action movie genre to be more distracting and a greater barrier to enjoyment.)

Let's go a little deeper into the relationship between singers and audiences in music drama.

Performers and Audiences in Music Drama

Public solo singing is a performance and therefore something set apart from ordinary life. Does it follow that all song performances – whether part of a dramatic production or not – can be understood in the same way? If this is so, then this chapter on song and drama is redundant. Yet as I hinted earlier, singing a song *in propria persona* seems to me different from singing while playing a character. Frank Sinatra is not singing as "Frank Sinatra" when his character "Chip" in *On the Town* bursts into song. And that is not the only difference between Sinatra-as-himself and Sinatra-as-Chip. Like songs, musical dramas are "works for performance," and, as such, they call for interpretation.[13] Yet unlike songs, where the interpretation is largely up to the singer or worked out between the singer and a music arranger or producer, the songs within music dramas are embedded within the interpretation of the work as a whole. As an established solo performer, Sinatra notoriously had a great deal of control over his music. Yet in singing as Chip he was constrained by some of the decisions already made by Gene Kelly and Stanley Donen, the directors of the film *On the Town*.

In Chapter 3 I argued that singing was at once social, cultural, and artistic, and that what a singer does and is understood as doing depends on both the singer's expectations and the audience's expectations. Considering song in the context of music drama brings in the additional element of the dramatic. You might recall that Adam Smith saw elements of acting in all song performance. All singers who perform works intended for performance may need to convey emotions they do not feel and a narrative perspective that they do not share. However, singers in dramas (and, to some extent, singers who perform songs from music dramas in concert) have an additional task. They must also convey character. Elements which convey character in music drama are not so different from the elements drawn upon in theatre more generally. These include costume and make-up, ways of moving on stage, gestures (large and small), facial expressions, vocal inflections, etc. But, in addition to these, character in music drama is developed and conveyed musically, through the melody and words of song, through the accompanying music, and through the details of vocal performance.

I have argued before that all successful vocal performances convey something beyond a text. For successful music drama performances, part of that "something else" is character. Singing in music drama can be a way both of revealing character and of developing character. A soprano singing the role of Tatiana in Tchaikovsky's *Eugene Onegin* and a soprano singing one of Tatiana's arias on stage both have to convey something of Tatiana's character: her youth and naivety in the earlier scenes, and her maturity and resolve in the final scenes. The opera performer has more resources than the concert singer, but also faces greater expectations. The opera singer typically has greater freedom of movement and a wider scope of action. He or she must also work within the dramatic constraints set by the director and the production design. The style of performance derisively referred to as "park and bark" – where a singer would stand still and sing rather than move around on stage – is increasingly a thing of the past. More and more, opera singers are expected to be proficient actors as well as singers.

Take, for example, Tatiana's "letter scene" and her aria that begins, "Let me die, but first ... " ("Puskai pogibnu ia, no prezhde ... ."). The scene is traditionally staged in Tatiana's bedroom. The young woman is overcome by emotion at having met and fallen in love with Onegin, and writes a letter to him declaring her love. In the Metropolitan Opera's 1997 production, Renée Fleming sang the role of Tatiana in what appears to be a bedroom (there is a bed), yet the stage is covered with fallen leaves.[14] The Met's 2013 production with Anna Netrebko sets the same scene in the sunroom where earlier action had taken place.[15] (Although in the clip available on the internet, the stage is so dark that it isn't readily apparent where we are.)[16] There are only limited props in both cases and limited possibilities for action. Both sopranos write letters; Fleming picks up and scatters some of the leaves, and Netrebko writhes a bit on the floor. Tatiana Monogarova, who starred in the Bolshoi Opera's production, plays the scene in what appears to be a large drawing room, dominated by a huge table with chairs. This gives her a greater scope of action: she mimes drinking a cup of tea, pushes the table away, scatters chairs, and eventually (it seemed inevitable) stands on top of the table.[17] (I fear that I may have made her performance sound silly; it is actually very affecting.) But what makes Monogarova's performance different from the other two is the decision that she sing the aria as if to an imaginary Onegin. While perhaps some viewers will find this to be excessively literal, for me it effectively underscores important aspects of Tatiana's character. She is highly impressionable and imaginative, so much so that she actually "sees" Onegin in her mind's eye.

Finally, compare these three performances with that of Khibla Gerzmava, singing the same aria in concert with the National Philharmonic Orchestra of Russia.[18] Without props or costume or set design, and with her actions limited to gestures, she manages to convey something of Tatiana. Some of her success can be attributed to the power of Tchaikovsky's music, yet we should not overlook the contribution made by Gerzmava's expressive performance. I can imagine a less skilled soprano who would fail to make Tatiana come alive for us. What Gerzmava does seems, on the one hand, less demanding than what the other three sopranos do. She gives us a "snapshot" of Tatiana and does not have to think about the character's development. The other singers have to make Tatiana in the opening scenes recognizably the same character as the more mature Tatiana of the later scenes. And Gerzmava does not have to situate her performance within a dramatic context developed by others. Yet, on the other hand, Gerzmava's performance might be seen as more challenging, as she lacks the resources (props, costumes, etc.) and the freedom of action of the other singers.

Within the community of opera fans there are debates about the relative importance of the dramatic component. When I discussed "hybrid" artworks in the second chapter, I said that opera was a hybrid of drama and music, and that there was something a little perverse about closing one's eyes and ignoring the dramatic component. While this seemed obvious to me, not everyone agrees. For them, opera is all about the music and shutting out the action on stage so as to focus on the music might be perfectly reasonable. Jerry Fodor expresses the opinion "widely held among a certain type of opera-lover" that the art of an opera director is to "disappear."[19] In other words, a highly personal or idiosyncratic dramatic setting is inappropriate. And here, making a similar point, is Kivy on acting in opera:

> We all know that singers are seldom good actors and actresses; that is just a statistical fact. But even in the rare instance, it is a mistake to indulge the talent except sparingly. And this for two obvious reasons. In the first place, because it is impossible to sing well if you are "saw[ing] the air too much with your hand" and transacting too much stage business. In the second, and more important, because *opera is in its most essential aspects a heard art, not a seen one*, and too much acting *distracts* from its *essentially* musical nature.[20] (Emphasis added.)

I will set aside Kivy's remark about good singers seldom being good actors, as it turns both on what we mean by "good" acting and on the comparison set proposed. From my perspective, there seems to be a consensus that acting in opera is getting better, and many argue that innovative stagings of old favorites have helped attract new fans. I also propose to set aside his contention that opera is "in its most essential aspects" a heard art. I disagree with Kivy on this, yet I don't feel that I have the argumentative resources or that this is the place to discuss the "essence" of opera. For one thing, I would frame the issue differently, as I suspect opera is best characterized historically rather than in terms of essential features. And if I am mistaken in this, and there really is an essence of opera, I would rather leave its characterization to opera's most devoted fans – the kind of people who spend much of their disposable income and free time chasing productions of Wagner's *Ring* cycle, for example.

What I find most interesting and fruitful in Kivy's remarks is his conviction that too much acting (or bad acting) "distracts" the audience. I said earlier that, to take pleasure in a performance, audiences need to be "convinced" and that incongruities within a performance threaten to distract their attention. Which elements of a performance will or will not distract an audience depend on their expectations, among other factors. Kivy is certainly correct that bad acting can distract an audience. For the type of audience member for whom opera is essentially a heard art, a very physical performance, like the one by Monogarova, might indeed prove distracting. Yet audience members new to opera and more familiar with the conventions of musical theatre might find the "park and bark" style to be distracting.

What about other factors, such as a singer's physical appearance? Debates about singers' physical appearance – about whether a specific performer has the right look for a character – reveal contrasting perspectives on the nature of opera and different audience expectations. Different values and different conceptions of opera underlie differences of opinion about singers' physical appropriateness for a role. These debates parallel the debates about non-traditional stagings. If opera is conceived as essentially a musical experience, as something to be heard, then a singer's appearance should not make a difference. For those who think of opera as a theatrical experience, the director's dramatic vision may be an important aspect of that experience. Someone who approaches opera primarily as music may well be distracted by an innovative staging, even one that is done well and otherwise effectively. The more that opera is conceived along the lines of a hybrid of music and theatre, the more things like the staging and a singer's physical appropriateness for the role become relevant considerations. And the further one moves from grand opera on the continuum of music drama, the more relevant are the non-musical aspects of a production. There may be some plausibility in treating *La Bohème* as an example of a heard art. At least, coherent arguments can be made for and against treating it in this way. But there is much less plausibility in treating *Rent* (which borrows liberally from *La Bohème*) as an essentially musical experience.

These different approaches to opera (with differing audience expectations of singers) are evident in nearly every controversy over singers' physical appearance. Take, for example, the controversy in 2004 when soprano Deborah Voigt was fired from a production of Strauss' *Ariadne auf Naxos* at Covent Garden. Apparently the director thought that Voigt was too heavy to look good in the little black dress that was part of his staging concept.[21] Critics countered that Voigt's unquestioned skill as a singer and interpreter of Strauss should be considered as more important than her physical appearance. As baritone Thomas Quasthoff said around the time, "The fuss about what singers look like is disgusting. ... No one thinks Deborah Voigt looks like a straw, but if a dress doesn't fit her, make a new one. I've worked with her and she's a wonderful artist. The way she has been treated [by Covent Garden] is disgusting. Disgusting."[22] Yet even opera singers differ on the relative importance of singers' physical appearance. Here is soprano Natalie Dessay, speaking on the convention that "mature" singers play the roles of much younger characters: "Is it reasonable? Is it believable? Is it nice? I don't think so."[23]

I discuss singers' physical appearance because appearance is a component of public persona. I hesitated a long time before deciding to write about this, but in the end I thought that the topic could not be avoided if I was interested in audience experience and the expectations that shape experience. I hesitated for a number of reasons. For one thing, the public discourse about such matters is impoverished, to say the least. Female singers are criticized for their appearance far more often than are male singers, and some of the commentators are just plain mean. For another thing, physical appearance is difficult to talk about in an insightful and respectful way, as it is mixed up with issues of personal preferences, sexual desire, cultural norms, race, and even human biology. Moreover, it is naïve to think of human beauty as reducible to physical appearance. In drama, in particular, it is difficult to separate the effects of physical appearance from other components such as stage presence, personal charisma, acting skill, and vocal ability.

I ultimately decided to write about physical appearance when a personal experience made me realize the impact it can have on an audience. When I planned to write about musical theatre, one of the musicals I decided to focus on was *Rent*. I watched the movie of the Broadway production and attended a live performance of it in Toronto. The character Maureen (a parallel to Musetta in *La Bohème*) is supposed to be drop-dead gorgeous. Men and women alike desire her and are supposed to be transfixed by her beauty. The Toronto actor who played Maureen was not believable as such a person. I felt a sense of incongruity whenever anyone referred to Maureen's "hotness" and desirability, and this sense of incongruity often took me out of the drama and out of the theatrical experience. I wondered if this simply meant that I was shallow, and maybe it does. But I think there is something interesting going on, in addition to my personal failings. It wasn't that the actress was unattractive. Rather, she seemed unable to convey the charisma and desirability that was supposedly her character's birthright. She couldn't inhabit the role, whether because she was not attractive to the degree of her character or because of her lack of acting ability.

Speaking of singers' public persona more generally (rather than about physical appearance in particular) I suspect that the elements I discussed with regard to popular and jazz singers also apply to singers who work in music drama. A singer's public persona is the face, body, and personal history that he or she presents to an audience, and it is conveyed through clothing and accessories, repertoire, and the statements and activities reported by the media or circulated among fans. Like other singers, those whose focus is in music drama may be obliged to create and promote a compelling persona. Stars sell tickets. Singers who, because of name recognition, can get people into the theatre or the opera house will have more options to work with the best orchestras and directors, and to perform in the kinds of works that they find most meaningful.

Given that singers in music drama have incentives to put forward a compelling public persona, how does this affect audiences? Can having a strong public persona (or a "star" image) conflict with the successful execution of a dramatic role? Can an audience watch "Chip" in *On the Town* and forget that they are also watching Sinatra? Would they even want to do so?

These are difficult questions, but the film business offers some clues. Actors with strong and distinctive star personas do indeed get typecast playing certain kinds of characters, and it can be difficult for audiences to relate to them outside of this persona. Some actors strive to demonstrate versatility while others become reconciled to playing variations on a theme. Cary Grant is a good example. He developed the persona of an urbane, debonair leading man. Today, even if you see him in one of his earlier films made before this persona solidified, it is difficult to see him as anyone other than the "Cary Grant" of his most famous films. Yet Grant's fans would probably not have had it otherwise. There is a thrill in seeing a recognizable actor play a character, especially a familiar character such as Hamlet or a well-known type such as a romantic comedy lead. Similarly, in opera, seeing a star persona sing a role is a winning combination – it is *him* or *her* playing Don Giovanni or Tosca or whomever. Seeing a star adds an element to the audience's experience and provides material for reflection. How does her "Tosca" compare to her "Violetta"? The soprano Maria Callas is praised for her acting ability. But for audiences who were lucky enough to see her in her prime, did she really "disappear" into her roles? Would they have wanted her to?

"Seasons of Love"

When an opera singer performs an aria from an opera as a concert piece it is usually obvious what is going on. That is, audiences recognize that the piece has been excerpted from a larger context, and that the singer is portraying a character. The singer may be more or less successful at conveying elements of the original character without the resources of musical theatre.

A great many jazz standards originated as songs in music drama: "It Never Entered My Mind" (which I wrote about in the Preface), "Summertime," "All the Things You Are," and many others. For most of these songs, I would venture, audiences no longer recognize their roots in theatre, and singers no longer attempt to convey elements of the original character who sang the song in the drama. If the characters and the dramas are no longer familiar to audiences, what would be the point of attempting to convey character? It would add little to the audience's experience. Other songs, because they are more recent or because of their lyrics, are recognizable as lifted from a dramatic context. Even someone who wasn't familiar with the musical *Evita* would likely suspect that "Don't Cry For Me Argentina" was from a play or film. Singing about Argentina without some kind of larger context is just too strange, especially when the performer seems to have no obvious connection to South America. Singers who perform such songs presumably have to think about whether they will perform the song as a work in its own right, or whether they will try to convey elements of the original character and dramatic context.

These musings on performance within a dramatic context extend the discussion that I have pursued now for several chapters: What is it to perform a song? I have chosen to focus on the song "Seasons of Love" from the musical *Rent* because I think it raises these questions in interesting ways. *Rent* (as likely everyone knows) is a hugely successful rock musical loosely based on Puccini's *La Bohème*. The composer, Jonathan Larson, died tragically of an undiagnosed heart condition on the eve of the show's off-Broadway premiere. He was posthumously awarded three Tony awards and the Pulitzer Prize for Drama. The song "Seasons of Love" is (as far as I know) the only song from the play to have a life of its own. It is an ensemble piece and has become a favorite of amateur choirs and school groups.

In the play's original conception, "Seasons of Love" was to be sung by the cast of assembled characters during the funeral of Angel, a young drag queen who dies of AIDS. At the original premiere of *Rent* the cast sang the song at the beginning of the show in order to pay their respects to Larson who had died the day before. In current performances, "Seasons of Love" is sung at the beginning of the second act, although I'm not sure how this practice came about. I've seen *Rent* a couple of times and I'm never sure what is going on when this song is performed. While the performers are presumably in character for the song, they also form a chorus commenting on the action thus far and setting us up for the action to come. They seem to me in this respect not so different from an operatic chorus. I also find it striking that the main solo part is given to a performer who plays two minor characters – "Mrs. Jefferson" and "Woman with bags." I've always wondered whether this has dramatic significance. Which character is singing the solo, or is she supposed to be singing as a generic "Everywoman"? Or perhaps I am over-thinking this and the producers, realizing that they had a wonderful and under-utilized singer in Gwen Stewart, decided to give her a prominent part in the song. If this was the case, it would not be so different from traditional practices in opera, when composers sometimes wrote parts with specific singers in mind.

Like the many amateur groups who have performed "Seasons of Love," the original cast of *Rent* has also performed the song outside of its dramatic context. Most famously, they sang it at the 1996 Democratic Convention, adding some new, politically relevant lyrics.[24] The performers were not in costume for this performance and were presumably singing as themselves. When the cast sang the song on opening night, as a tribute to Larson, were they in character or not? Presumably, there were elements of both. On the one hand, they sang the song as a personal tribute; on the other hand, one way to honor a composer is to sing as a character he created.

"Seasons of Love" is associated with AIDS because one character in *Rent* dies of the disease and several others are HIV positive. The song is a *memento mori*. The theme of "measuring" life reminds us that life comes to an end, as only finite things can be measured. The song asks, what counts in a life? Is it simply the length of time one spends on earth, or is it something else? Questions about the value of life are also about the meaning of life. Yet although the lyrics refer to serious, if not dark themes, the song is anything but depressing. The answer to "how do you measure a life?" is "measure in love" and the lyrics stress the importance of remembering and celebrating those who have died. The music is relentlessly upbeat and the singers begin clapping in time with the music just over halfway through. (The Broadway audience in the clip I saw starts clapping along after the first verse.)

The question of *who* is singing (a character or a performer *in propria persona*) is intertwined with the question of *for whom* the singer sings. Although "Seasons of Love" is not an explicitly religious song, its weighty themes and emphasis on love give it a religious feel. This is enhanced by the addition of musical elements usually found in Gospel music: handclaps and the soloists' melisma. One way we can understand the song and the issues it raises is to compare it to an earlier and perhaps remote tradition of singing. I have in mind the medieval tradition of songs that were also prayers.[25] When medieval choristers sang a motet, they were singing for the glory of God and for themselves, as if they sang with pure hearts their prayers would be answered. They also sang on behalf of the patron who had commissioned the motet and for any listeners, as hearing a sung prayer should offer the same benefits as saying or singing a prayer oneself. Finally, the singers sang for the composer, as their voices allowed his prayers to be heard once again from beyond the grave. If this analogy is relevant, then those who sing "Seasons of Love" are singing for themselves (for the love of song), for their audience, and for Larson, whether they sing in character or not.

Perhaps the tuneful and catchy "Seasons of Love" cannot bear the weighty comparison I have proposed. Yet I am convinced that some of the song's popularity stems from its engagement with serious themes like death and the meaning of life. Despite the prevailing silliness of popular culture, I believe that people want the chance to think through substantial and serious issues. And one of the ways to engage with such issues is through song. These thoughts propel us onto our next topics: the meaning of song and why do we sing.

Notes

1 Leo Tolstoy, *What is Art?* trans. Aylmer Maude (Indianapolis: Hackett Publishing Co., 1996 [1896]), 13.

2 Tolstoy, *What is Art?* 14.

3 See Anthony Tommasini, "Critic's Notebook; 'Once in Love with Carmen'? Nope," *The New York Times,* January 24, 2000, www.nytimes.com/2000/01/24/theater/critic-s-notebook-once-in-love-with-carmen-nope.html (accessed December 9, 2014); and "Opera? Musical? Please Respect the Difference," *The New York*

Times, July 7, 2011, www.nytimes.com/2011/07/10/theater/musical-or-opera-the-fine-line-that-divides-them.html?pagewanted=all (accessed December 9, 2014).

4 Bernard Williams, *On Opera* (New Haven: Yale University Press, 2006), 134.

5 Levinson, "Song and Music Drama," in *The Pleasures of Aesthetics* (Ithaca: Cornell University Press, 1996), 57–59.

6 Robert Yanal, "Words and Music," *Journal of Philosophy* 78:4 (1981), 189.

7 Yanal, "Words and Music," 188–89. Italics added.

8 Peter Kivy, "Realistic Song in the Movies," *Journal of Aesthetics and Art Criticism* 71:1 (2013), 75–80.

9 Edward Cone, "The World of Opera and its Inhabitants," in *Music: A View from Delft: Selected Essay* ed. Robert P. Morgan (Chicago, 1989), 125–38.

10 Peter Kivy, "Opera Talk: A Philosophical 'Phantasie'," *The Fine Art of Repetition: Essays in the Philosophy of Music* (Cambridge: Cambridge University Press, 1993), 148.

11 David Rosen, "Cone's and Kivy's 'World of Opera'," *Cambridge Opera Journal* 4:1 (1992), 63.

12 Retold in Aljean Harmetz, *Round up the Usual Suspects: The making of Casablanca – Bogart, Bergman, and World War II* (Hyperion, 1993), 185.

13 My understanding is indebted to Paul Thom, *For An Audience: A Philosophy of the Performing Arts* (Philadelphia: Temple University Press, 1993).

14 www.youtube.com/watch?v=K0kvyzfmzHs (accessed December 9, 2014).

15 Described in Anthony Tommasini, "A Fight for Love, in the Met and Out," *The New York Times,* September 24, 2013, www.nytimes.com/2013/09/25/arts/music/love-and-conflict-in-the-19th-century-and-the-21st.html?pagewanted=all (accessed December 9, 2014).

16 www.youtube.com/watch?v=d56MMagyMXs

17 www.youtube.com/watch?v=cibwQFbwEPs

18 www.youtube.com/watch?v=HPzRVqtgxWo

19 Jerry Fodor quoted in Paul Thom, "Opera," in Theodore Gracyk and Andrew Kania (eds), *Routledge Companion to the Philosophy of Music* (New York: Routledge, 2011), 453. The remark about "a certain type of opera lover" is Thom's.

20 Kivy, "Opera Talk," 156.

21 Anthony Tommasini, "With Surgery, Soprano Sheds a Brünnhilde Body," *The New York Times,* March 27, 2005, www.nytimes.com/2005/03/27/arts/music/27voig.html?pagewanted=1&_r=0&adxnnlx=1399831204-34H3PhwvDxNAZ/Bh LcKFqA (accessed December 9, 2014).

22 Fiona Maddocks, "Thomas Quasthoff Speaks *Very* Frankly," *Evening Standard* [London] February 25, 2005, http://web.archive.org/web/20050305114834/http://www.andante.com/article/article.cfm?id=25239 (accessed December 9, 2014).

23 Rebecca Mead, "The Actress," *The New Yorker,* March 2, 2009, 58.

24 http://youtu.be/WlOWRrXqTr4

25 Bonnie J. Blackburn, "For Whom Do the Singers Sing?" *Early Music* 25 (1997), 593–609.

9 Meaning

Songs in Performance

How to Think About the Meaning of Songs

When I first raised the issue of song meaning, back in Chapter 1, I deferred the discussion. At this point everything is finally in place to discuss song meaning. What is the meaning of a song and where is it located? In a song's text, in its music, in their conjunction, or in the tension between them?

These questions are too broad. We've seen that there are different kinds of songs, and how to approach the meaning of a particular song depends very much on the kind of song it is. Back in Chapter 3, I proposed a three-part, functional classification of songs. First were "works for performance," specifically intended to be performed, often in a formal setting.[1] These include art songs, songs in opera and music drama, jazz standards, and the songs recorded by professional singers for a mass audience. Second were songs intended for "participation-performance" or communal singing, with the "audience" and the performers being one. Such songs include national anthems, hymns, camp-fire songs, and many folk songs. Even when only one person performs such a song, he or she does so less *for* an audience than *on behalf* of an audience.[2] Finally, some songs are best understood as "functional" songs because they serve specific practical or cultural purposes. Examples include lullabies, mnemonic songs, work songs, and laments. The account of musical meaning I develop in this chapter applies only to the first type of song – those songs that are works for performance and that are sung in performance.

Just to give a hint of what is to come, I will argue that meaning is a product of three factors: a song's text; its music; and the performance context. Song meaning is co-created by performers and listeners, within specific contexts.

More About Works for Performance

What sets apart works for performance from other types of songs? They have a different teleology than do those songs which are not works for performance, and they also have a different teleology from other artworks which are not works for performance. By this I mean that they are created for different purposes and have different goals. Works for performance are understood, both by creators and by audiences, as calling for a certain kind of "playful" attention.[3] Such works for performance are not simply "transmitted" or neutrally "conveyed" to an audience. They are performed, that is, enacted, embodied, put on, staged. Works for performance are occasions for artistic actions in front of audiences. It follows that the interpretation of a work as a prelude to performing it is a different kind of activity than other kinds of artistic interpretation. To interpret a poem, say, is one kind of activity. There has been a lot of philosophical discussion over what is the proper goal of this activity, and to what extent the author's likely intentions for the work have to be discerned and respected. But whatever one is doing in interpreting a literary text, to interpret that same text as a prelude to singing the song of which it is part is a different kind of activity. These different activities have different goals and different success criteria. It is an open question whether a true interpretation of a text – whatever we decide will count as such – will necessarily also be an interpretation that is conducive to a successful performance of that text.

What I am underlining here is the difference between critical and performative interpretations. Take a standard literary work, one that is not also a work for performance. Here I would endorse something like the position defended by Robert Stecker. He proposes that an artwork has whatever meaning that it has due to a combination of "the actual intentions of artists and the conventions in place when the work is created."[4] For example, Shakespeare's *Richard III* is not a critique of fascism; to insist that it is would be a misinterpretation. However, if a theatre or film director mounted a production of *Richard III* such that it was meant to convey a critique of fascism, that is another matter. It would not be legitimate to argue that the director misunderstood the play. Rather, she staged the play in such a way that it took on new meanings for contemporary audiences. The meaning of the work in performance may be legitimately different from the meaning of the work understood as a text.

These reflections on interpretation lead me to two further thoughts with respect to the meaning of those works of music which are works for performance. First, while composers create works, they do not fully determine the meaning of those works. The meaning of a work in performance can only be co-created – by composers, performers, and audiences together. Again, this is because of the kind of thing a work for performance is. In creating a work for performance, a composer offers something whose teleology can be fulfilled only by the agency of other people – musicians who will perform the work and audiences who will listen. Composers can offer more or less detailed instructions to performers, but they cannot determine the actions of performers. Performers can intend that audiences interpret their actions and the sounds that they produce in certain ways, but they cannot determine how, exactly, audiences will respond, and the meanings that audiences will find in those performances.

My second thought about meaning is one that I have been defending throughout the book. Namely, linguistic models are of limited application in understanding and explaining meaning in music. They are of limited application even where we might expect them to be most helpful – in explaining the meaning of songs. Rhetorical models of music, which originated in ancient Greek ideas about the character-forming power of *mousike*, dominated theorizing about musical meaning until the early modern period and continue to be significant today. Their influence remains evident in what might be called the "propositional" model of song meaning. According to this model, which may be tacitly accepted rather than explicitly endorsed, the meaning of a song can be reduced to the meaning of its verbal text. The propositional model becomes unsatisfactory when we take a closer look at song texts, as we did in Chapter 1. We saw there that songs are a form of oral communication and as such are subject to the burdens and limitations of oral communication. Song texts tend to be highly redundant, predictable, and often formulaic; they convey a low density of information and trade in familiar simplifications. However, if the meaning of a song is the meaning of its text, then it becomes difficult to explain the endurance of songs and singing across time and space. Song is music and text is not, and song is not a very efficient means for conveying propositional meaning. While most songs do convey a text, their meaning cannot be reduced to the propositional content of that text.

Let me expand a little upon the claim that meanings are co-created. A fully adequate account of meaning in songs requires an understanding of meaning as social and as emerging in the interactions between a work, a performer, and an audience. Songs, as works for performance, are under-determined and have varying degrees of ontological "thickness." While under-determination is characteristic of all songs (indeed, of many works for performance), it is especially relevant for those musical genres in which performers have a great deal of interpretive freedom. Listeners experience songs through performances. Performers "flesh out" songs and interpret them for audiences, who, depending on their expectations, may have qualitatively different experiences. What a singer intends to communicate or transmit in performance may or may not be received by listeners. Composers and singers can only *intend* that their works and their actions be understood in certain ways. They cannot *stipulate* that audiences take away the meanings that they intend. Audiences are not sponges; audiences come to performances with personal and cultural histories and with certain expectations. They may or may not have the kind of experience that performers intend them to have. But the experiences of listeners must have a place in understanding the meaning of performances, as a work for performance has not fulfilled its teleology until it is, in fact, performed. To insist otherwise is to have a mistaken view about the nature of songs as works for performance.

Understanding performance meaning in the way that I have proposed – as emerging from social interactions rather than from performers' intentions and surrounding contextual features – helps us better understand what happens in performances. In the rest of this chapter I'll illustrate these claims about the meaning of song performances by means of analyzing some examples from different performance traditions.

"Chattanooga Choo Choo"

The performance of this much-loved WWII-era song by Glenn Miller and his band is a highlight of the 1941 film *Sun Valley Serenade*. The band plays the song through, before Tex Beneke and the Modernaires sing a short intro (which I believe was specific to the film), and then sing the song in its entirety, trading lines back and forth. They take their seats. The camera pans over to part of the set that has been made to look like a train station, and we see Dorothy Dandridge and the Nicholas Brothers emerge. Together they sing the song again, trading lines, and omitting the final verse. They all dance together for a few minutes, then Dandridge exits the stage and the Nicholas Brothers work their exuberant magic.[5]

"Chattanooga Choo Choo" is an example of two different thematic strains in American popular music: songs about trains, and songs that express nostalgia for the south. The song is imbued with the racial attitudes of its time, and one can only assume that the "boy" addressed at the beginning of the song is an African-American adult ("Pardon me, boy/ Is that the Chattanooga Choo Choo?"). African-Americans' feelings about the south, and their attitudes towards it, must have been complex, not to say ambivalent. The year of the film's release, 1941, was the beginning of the Second Great Migration, in which African-Americans in large numbers left the south for the north and the west. Of course, none of this is hinted at in the words of the song, or in any of the performances, although perhaps it is a telling omission that the African-American performers do not sing the exultant final verse, in which the narrator plans to tell his beloved that he will cease to "roam" and that Chattanooga is "home."

Even when the two groups of performers – Tex Beneke and the Modernaires and Dorothy Dandridge and the Nicholas Brothers – sing basically the same lyrics, the meaning created by their respective performances is different. This is clearest in the following lines from the second verse:

> Dinner in the diner
> Nothing could be finer
> Than to have your ham an' eggs
> In Carolina

In the Jim Crow south of the pre-Civil Rights era, independent African-American travelers did not typically eat in the dining cars of trains, and, when they did, a curtain separated them from the other passengers. Knowing this, as we do, and as white and black audiences of the time presumably did, makes the two performances of these lines different in character and import. When the white performers sing there is no distance between themselves and the lines; the literal meaning of the text is amplified by the joy in their voices: They are living the good life, eagerly anticipating a triumphant return home. When Dandridge and the Nicholas Brothers sing the same lines, and when one knows something of the contemporary cultural mores, the reminder is inescapable: These singers would not exactly be a welcome presence in the dining car. To my eyes and ears, their polished performances do not betray any ambivalence they may have felt in singing about segregated dining cars, or singing in an un-nuanced way about the south. Did audiences in 1941 register any incongruity or even irony in African-Americans singing the praises of dining cars where their presence was actively discouraged? Or was any strangeness subsumed in the fantasy atmosphere of a Hollywood movie? I don't know. Yet a sensitive audience, then or now, would likely be alert to the clues, hesitancies, tension, in the performers' voices and bodies, and these patterns of attention will shape their response to the performance.

The two performances of "Chattanooga Choo Choo" in *Sun Valley Serenade* illustrate how a song's meaning in performance can be shaped by the physical and social identities of the singers and by audience expectations. The audience's understanding of the cultural context and their awareness of the singers' identities shape their expectations and guide their attention in tangible ways, and make certain moments of the performance more salient than others.

"Pretty Polly"[6]

This traditional Appalachian murder ballad has antecedents in several earlier British ballads. It is a first-person account by a man who murders his lover. The "well-established formula" of the murder ballad is as follows: "A young woman is lured away from home by her lover to a secluded spot on the pretext of marriage or discussing marriage; presumably, she is pregnant. Once they go away together he kills her either to solve the problem of the pregnancy or to punish her for her sexual excesses. Sometimes he announces his murderous intentions to her, and we hear her pleas for mercy. After stabbing, shooting, or beating her to death he disposes of her body in a shallow grave or a river."[7]

For this example I propose to focus on style of performance, rather than on performers' identities. Fans of Appalachian music may face a dilemma shared by fans of opera, rap, and some rock music: how to take pleasure in the music while being aware of its violence and misogyny?[8] If violence against women were no longer a social problem, one might be tempted to explain away the song as the product of a less-enlightened era. The performance practices of traditional Appalachian music tend to magnify these tensions for contemporary listeners. The convention is to sing these songs dispassionately, with singers bringing little of their own personalities into the performance. As one traditional ballad singer puts it, "You have to put yourself *behind* the song. By that I mean get out of the way of it."[9] Another singer compares this impersonal vocal stance to that of a "disinterested newspaper writer reporting just the facts."[10] Contemporary audiences unfamiliar with these conventions may mistakenly form the impression that the singers condone, or at least do not challenge, the violence described in the songs. Contemporary performers have employed a number of strategies to undermine or resist the violence in "Pretty Polly," and in so doing modify the meaning of the song for their audiences. Some simply give up the traditional performance style or omit some of the more gruesome verses. Ralph Stanley recorded the song as a duet with Patty Loveless.[11] Other performers have incorporated instrumental counter-melodies to represent Polly and give her a voice, albeit wordless.

Listeners may find some of these strategies to be more or less successful at resisting the violence in the song. We might analyze the details of each performance and give reasons in defense of the performances we find most successful.[12] Instead let us simply imagine two different performances: One that listeners hear as condoning the violence in "Pretty Polly" and another that listeners hear as successfully resisting it. Despite being performances of the same song, the two performances would have different meanings, emerging from different patterns of interaction between the song, the performance, and the audience. The first audience hears a song about how a woman who should have known better meets a gruesome end. The second audience hears a song about social injustice.

A possible objection arises right away. Listeners who have heard the first performance as condoning the violence in "Pretty Polly" may have simply misunderstood the singer's intentions because they are unfamiliar with the traditional performance practices. So what we have here is a case of *misunderstanding* the meaning of a performance, rather than the co-creation of a different meaning. Let us assume that the listeners have indeed misunderstood the performer's intentions. The singer performed in a self-effacing manner with the intention of better conveying the narrative of the song. The naïve audience experienced the performance as an endorsement of violence as a form of social control.

However, while the audience may have misunderstood the performer's *intentions*, it does not follow that they misunderstood the *performance*. The audience heard what they heard – a dispassionate rendition of a murder ballad – and that created for them a certain meaning. To be sure, this meaning was not the one that the performer intended to convey. Misunderstanding others' intentions is an all too common occurrence. Performers' intentions are only one element that goes to create performance meaning. While performers can intend that their audiences interpret the performance as, say, unostentatious, rather than as neutral regarding violence against women, they cannot stipulate that audiences understand it in that way.

"Heidenröslein" (Little Heath-rose)[13]

Goethe's poem "Heidenröslein" recounts the story of a boy who spies a beautiful red rose and picks it, despite the rose's protestations and threats to prick him with her thorns. It has been set to music many times, most notably by Schubert. As Lawrence Kramer writes, "The poem tells a simple story, but no one would be so simple as to think it's about a flower. Obviously, it's about a girl being *deflowered*."[14] Schubert's song is an example of a then-familiar type – an art song that is meant to sound like folk music. (In fact I've seen it several times referred to, erroneously, as a German folk song.) Schubert's song is simple and straightforward in feeling; the musical accompaniment does not draw attention to itself. The meaning of Goethe's text, to quote Kramer again, is that "girls like the little red rose have got to yield to the sexual insistence of boys, and that even if this involves a certain violence there is no use making a fuss about it. That's life."[15] Kramer argues that Schubert's setting of the song seems to endorse the text: "Schubert's song takes this cynical-worldly view and makes positive pleasure of it; the prevailing mood of the music, its warm, lilting lyricism, is responsive to the beauty of the rose but perfectly indifferent to her suffering."[16]

Now, "Heidenröslein" is extremely singable; indeed Kramer calls it a "perfect gift to amateur vocalists."[17] But its singability – and its overall stance of indifference to the rose – is subtly undermined. Three times, a lingering and exposed high G in the song's refrain "freezes the musical action" as if the singer were feeling compassion for the rose.[18] It is not difficult to see how different meanings can be created in performance by how the singer handles that high G. If a singer doesn't linger long enough, the effect may be too subtle to register. If he lingers too long, the effect will be at odds with the simple and straightforward character of the rest of the song. And amateur singers who strain, however slightly, to reach and hold the pitch might remind their audience that they are listening to art music, not to a folk song within the range of most singers.

Like so many cultural products, high and low, "Heidenröslein" has a presence on the internet. One can hear it sung by a number of great vocalists. The performance by the Vienna Boys Choir almost makes one believe that the song might be about a flower after all. Another singer takes an overly literal approach and sits behind a table on which stands, wait for it, a vase with a red rose.[19] At one time it was possible to see the scene from Hitchcock's *Lifeboat* where the song is sung by the villainous Nazi U-boat captain, although the clip has been since removed. There is also a purposely (I think) ugly and tuneless rendition that is accompanied by an equally offputting animation sequence.[20] The ugliness of the singing and the visuals are perhaps meant to convey what the singer and the animator see as the ugliness and violence of the song and the attitudes it embodies.

How can meaning be co-created by audiences in the case of "Heidenröslein"? Different listeners will have different experiences of each performance. Take, at one extreme, a non-German speaker who enjoys the song as a purely musical construction. Her experience will be very different than that of another listener who fully understands the text. Listeners who understand the poem's text and its symbolism but are made uncomfortable by its implications are likely to resist, or at least feel conflicted by, the pleasures offered even by a polished and sensitive performance of Schubert's song. The attitudes to female sexuality that underlie Goethe's poem are not as widely endorsed today as they were in his time. Today they are anachronistic at best, and an apology for sexual violence at worst. Other listeners, who hear the song primarily as a expression of German high culture and therefore to be revered, are likely to be upset by the rejection of those values in the tuneless and "resisting" performance of the song.

An Objection

Someone might object that the account I have presented is too liberal. Not all performance choices are equally appropriate or legitimate. At least some ways of singing a song will misrepresent it or what it is about.[21]

First, I think it is clear that not all performance choices are equally appropriate. But performance choices may be inappropriate for a number of reasons. Singers may attempt to sing material that is out of their comfort range. They may perform without adequate practice. They may misunderstand a song's text. Or they may simply show poor musical judgment. But my concern here isn't to provide a way to adjudicate between different performances – my goal has been to show how the meaning of a song in performance is constructed.

Second, this objection seems to assume that the only goal (or perhaps the most important goal) of performance is to uncover the meaning of the text and to convey this meaning to an audience. This would be akin to the view that, in instrumental music, performers' primary duty is to convey the composer's intentions to an audience. This view may be the dominant conception of what performers are doing (or should be doing) when they perform musical works. I think it would be foolish to argue that the composers' intentions are unimportant or to be easily set aside. Yet conveying a composer's vision or conveying the literal meaning of a song text are not the *only* legitimate goals of performance. Performers may also wish to make works come alive for contemporary audiences, or to express themselves through musical works, or simply to provide for audiences the richest experience possible. If respecting a composer's intentions was the only goal of performance, then the best performance of a commercial work would be one that emphasized its commerciality – and this just seems mistaken to me.

So singers may perform songs with a view to conveying the meaning of a text – indeed, this may be what they do most of the time. But I don't think it follows that this is always what they should do. Before we judge a singer adversely for failing to convey the meaning of a particular text, we should ask ourselves if that was indeed her intention. It may not have been. And if we judge a particular performance poorly, this may be for other reasons than the singer's alleged failure to convey the meaning of a text. Performances can fail for any number of reasons.

In conclusion, let me return to general issues. The meaning of a performance is not transmitted from a composer to a performer to an audience, as one might transmit a package from Toronto to Washington by FedEx. Songs are not utterances or assertions whose meanings might be amenable to linguistic and pragmatic analysis. Those songs that are works for performance are not typically "uttered"; rather, they are *performed*, and performance implies an audience. The meanings of songs in performance are constituted by, or emerge within, the patterns of interaction between a work, a performer, and an audience.

A music performance is a social occasion and performers and audiences respond to one another. Singers perform differently for an audience of fans than they do for an audience of neophytes. They perform differently in their home towns than on the road. Sometimes it is obvious when a performer responds to an audience. Take the moment when Nina Simone, in the course of singing "Children Go Where I Send Thee," at the Village Gate in New York City, asks her listeners, "You ever been to a revival meeting?" On the recording of her performance you can just hear one of her musicians tell her, "They don't know nothing about that." She tells the audience: "Well you in one right now."[22] Simone, together with her band, is framing or contextualizing the song for an audience who is presumably ignorant about it. I suspect that she would not have felt the need to contextualize the song in the same way for a predominantly African-American audience or for an audience in the American south.

Other times, the way that performers respond to audiences is more subtle and harder to detect. Similarly, audiences respond to performers in both subtle and obvious ways. We have probably all had the experience of noticing when a speaker or performer has "lost" an audience – the shuffling of bodies in seats, the rustling of papers, the signs and sounds of inattention. Audience responses are, of course, not always so obvious. They may be quick, fleeting, and below the threshold of everyday awareness. Yet we must attend to them, and our theoretical structures must maintain a place for them, if we hope to understand how works in performance acquire meaning.

Notes

1 See Paul Thom, *For an Audience*, Chapter 1; and Stephen Davies, *Musical Works and Performances*, 20–25.
2 Victor Zuckerkandl, *Man the Musician* (Princeton: Princeton University Press, 1973), 27.
3 I owe this characterization of works for performance to Thom, *For an Audience*.
4 Robert Stecker, *Interpretation and Construction: Art, Speech, and the Law* (Malden, MA: Blackwell Publishing, 2003), 42.

5 http://youtu.be/kIQq1j1-AQU

6 My analysis here is indebted to Lydia Hamessley, "A Resisting Performance of an Appalachian Traditional Murder Ballad: Giving Voice to 'Pretty Polly'," *Women and Music* 9 (2005), 13–36.

7 Hamessley, "A Resisting Performance," 15.

8 Ted Gracyk discusses this issue in *I Wanna Be Me.*

9 Almeda Riddle, quoted in Hamessley, "A Resisting Performance," 18.

10 Sheila Kay Adams, quoted in Hamessley, "A Resisting Performance," 19.

11 See www.youtube.com/watch?v=3XV7mxfIIr0

12 As Hamessley does in "A Resisting Performance."

13 My analysis here is indebted to Lawrence Kramer, "Beyond Words and Music: An Essay on Songfulness," in *Musical Meaning: Towards a Critical History* (Berkeley and Los Angeles, CA: University of California Press, 2001), 51–67.

14 Kramer, "Beyond Words and Music," 55.

15 Kramer, "Beyond Words and Music," 62.

16 Kramer, "Beyond Words and Music," 62.

17 Kramer, "Beyond Words and Music," 58.

18 Kramer, "Beyond Words and Music," 62.

19 www.youtube.com/watch?v=XYjBNIl2fe4

20 www.youtube.com/watch?v=tONDZwQDAsM

21 I'm grateful to Stephen Davies for raising this objection.

22 Nina Simone, *Live at the Village Gate,* recorded in 1961, released in 1962. Produced by Cal Lampey on the Colpix Label.

10 Why Sing?

> Though the regions of the body most responsible for singing are easily monitored, singing itself does not calcify or clot; it cannot be X-rayed or splinted, like our other breakable body parts. For the voice is not a body part at all.
>
> (Elena Passarello – essayist)[1]

Let me be the first to admit that "Why sing?" is a strange question. Yet consider this: singing is not like eating or sleeping. It fulfills no obvious physical need. We can make music without the voice, instrumental music having been "emancipated" from words centuries ago. When we must communicate, ordinary speech does the job more efficiently than song. However, despite its superfluous status, the practice of singing – both as a performing art and as a cultural practice – has not atrophied. Indeed it seems to be thriving. Composers continue to set words to music and listeners persist in seeking out vocal music in all the genres in which it has a place. Song and singing have retained their importance. Why is this so?

"Why sing?" is the sort of question that not only will different people give different answers to, but different people will see themselves as answering different questions. And the question can certainly mean different things. "Why sing?" might mean:

Why sing (rather than speak)?
Why sing (and make singing central to your life)?
Why sing (why vocal music rather than instrumental)?
Why sing (in the choir rather than take up a different leisure activity)?
Why sing (around the campfire instead of tell stories)?
Why sing (along with the car radio when no one can hear)?
Why sing (in the shower when you can't hold a tune)?

Singing is sometimes a means to an end or a way of pursuing other goals. This is "singing for one's supper" (with "supper" here referring to any extrinsic end). As I recounted in the Preface, I originally signed up for a singing class because I thought it would help me use my voice more effectively in teaching large classes. Learning to sing has many non-musical benefits. The discipline and focus required can carry into other areas of life, as they do for students of musical instruments and for aspiring athletes. Singing (and making music generally) have been shown to contribute to overall well-being, most likely because participants form and maintain social connections with others. A U.K. study of 375 adults who either sang alone, sang in a choir, or played team sports found that all three activities contributed to psychological well-being, but choir singers experienced the greatest benefits.[2] Other studies have also shown an increase in subjective well-being for people who participate in choral singing, both among those who already enjoy good mental health as well as those with varying degrees of mental illness.[3]

While enjoying the benefits of singing may contribute to keeping people in choirs and attending singing lessons, I doubt that many take up singing simply *for the sake* of such benefits. In this, human beings are not unlike birds. Birdsong has been studied intensively for about 50 years, and a great deal is now known about its mechanisms, function, and ontogeny.[4] However, we don't actually know *why* birds sing. The standard functional explanations of birdsong are inadequate. While some birds sing "for their suppers" (to establish territories and attract mates), their songs are excessively complex and beautiful for these purposes. Even if it is the case that birdsong developed throughout evolution for functional reasons, it does not follow that birds now sing only because of evolutionary programming.[5] Might it be that some species of birds sing for their own enjoyment and have evolved the ability to appreciate melody?[6]

The decision to sing is rarely the outcome of a purely utilitarian calculus, I would guess, neither for birds nor for human beings. Here I discuss some (non-exclusive) reasons for singing.

Singing for Others (I): Because There Is an Audience

Vocal music has had a prominent place in the history of music and is an important component of contemporary popular music in nearly every genre. Some of the greatest music in any tradition is for voice or voices. People are usually exposed to vocal music at an early age, through live performances in schools and places of worship. As long as there is an audience for vocal music, there will be people willing to sing for others.

The popularity of singing and the enjoyment that many seem to get from listening to vocal music helps account for the success of television programs such as *The Voice*, the "Idol" series, and those that proclaim that some particular geographic location has "Got Talent." I find it interesting that in such programs some combination of expert opinion and popular vote is presumed to be the correct way to decide who is the "best" singer. These programs could be set up differently. The judging could be left to experts, with or without a live audience participating. Or performances could be recorded without an audience, and listeners could participate in judging by phone or internet. Instead, a live audience is made central and the audience's responses are turned into a significant part of the program's narrative.

A live audience that participates in the competition by judging enhances the social aspect of song performance. It emphasizes that this singing is *for others*. Musicians and listeners need one another. There is no music without performers, and no "performance" to an empty auditorium.

To sing for others is to offer them a gift. While still a young woman, the African-American contralto Marian Anderson wrote that she did not feel that her voice was her "personal property." Rather, she said, "it belongs to everybody. I do feel that I should make every effort to present it to the public in the best form possible."[7] Anderson's selflessness may have been extreme, even for a professional performer. But her remarks capture the dedication to one's art and to one's audience that is demanded of all performers, and perhaps more so of singers, whose instrument is their body.

Singing for Others (II): Because It Is a Way of Demanding Recognition

Not everyone who loves to sing wants to sing for others, but for those who do pursue singing for an audience, what does the desire to fill the role of "singer" amount to, and what kind of role is it? One can take up the role temporarily and for a limited time rather than making it a career. So let us not limit our thinking to professionals, but consider choristers, both those who aspire to sing solo parts and those happier as part of the chorus, as well as singers who participate in amateur musicals and talent shows. Let's even consider karaoke singers and the homeless man who sings for spare change outside the grocery store near where I live.

I have come to think that one answer to the question "Why sing?" connects in some more fundamental way with the nature and significance of the human voice and the desire for recognition. What kind of "recognition" am I talking about? I do not mean the acknowledgement by others that one is a good singer or has a beautiful voice. I have in mind something much more basic. I mean the acknowledgement by others of one's standing as a human being with basic dignity, as an equal to others in this regard, and as worthy of respect.

I feel comfortable making these rather grandiose claims about singing because there is something ineluctably human about the voice. Recall Gracyk's contention that the authorship of a song attaches to the gendered body of a singer, regardless of our knowledge of actual authorship.[8] We hear singers as agents, but in a stronger sense than we may hear other musicians as agents. As Cone has argued, one cannot help but interpret a vocalist as a protagonist, rather than as the player of an instrument, even when the singer produces nonsense syllables. A singer is heard as a human protagonist in a way that is not necessarily true of a trumpeter or violinist. Cone linked the listeners' sense of agency to something in the voice. As he put it, "For when the human voice sings, it demands to be heard, and when it is heard it demands recognition."[9] This quality of the human voice as demanding recognition also accounts for the plausibility of philosopher Mladen Dolar's observation that the impersonal or mechanically produced voice always has a touch of the uncanny.[10] We hear something that demands the recognition we would give to another human being, yet the sound has been produced mechanically.

With the human desire to be recognized comes the moral and social obligation to recognize others. But this is a recognition we may be reluctant to afford, the more so if we are obliged. Perhaps this is why singers, of all buskers, seem to me to have the potential to be particularly cringe-making. The obligation to recognize coincides with the desire to ignore and the result is generally discomfort.

Singing for Oneself: Because It Is a Way of Participating In the Arts

In Plato's *Republic*, Socrates and a group of men discuss the perfect city. Socrates first proposes a city in which everyone shares the work and all the basic necessities of life are met (369b–372e). The food is plain, but healthy. The people live in modest dwellings without decoration; their clothes keep them warm enough but are likewise plain and simple. Socrates says that such a city would be healthy and without strife. Glaucon, one of those present, angrily rejects Socrates' vision, saying that a city must have luxuries: spices to enhance food, fancy clothes, comfortable cushions, beautiful decorations, and so on. Socrates' "healthy" city, he says, is really a "City of Pigs."

There are a number of ways to interpret the exchange. The one which resonates most strongly for me is that the "healthy" city would not be suitable for human beings because we require something "extra" beyond basic sustenance.[11] A life of subsistence might be fine for animals such as pigs, but human beings have a need for the "luxuries" of art, beauty, and comfort. Paradoxically, while these things taken individually are luxuries and no one by itself is necessary to sustain life, some element of "luxury" is necessary for human society.

This inescapable aesthetic component in human life is evident both in the reception of art and in its creation. It also shows itself in the time and resources spent on activities that enhance aesthetic value but do not contribute directly to survival. Think of fashion and make-up, cooking that goes beyond the satisfaction of nutritional requirements, decorative gardening, and interior decorating. Even the world's poorest people decorate their dwellings. People seek a way to participate in creative life even when it is inconvenient and time-consuming. I play in a community concert band. We include lawyers, a police officer, an accountant, a graphic designer, and several business owners and teachers. Music brings us together every week. The time spent at rehearsal, concerts, and individual practice is time away from our families, from extra sleep, and from sometimes demanding work. In addition to playing, we also need to maintain our instruments, sell concert tickets, promote events, and sometimes drive to far-flung locations. Among my friends who do not play instruments, many have found other ways to participate in creative life. A couple of them write fiction, a scientist friend does theatre improv, a librarian I know is talented enough to have his photography shown in galleries, and many others display their photography on internet photo-sharing sites.

Not everyone who wants to sing wants to be a soloist, and singing with others in a choir is a way to enhance the aesthetic aspect of life. Singing in a choir is one of the most accessible ways to make music for others and to be surrounded by live music oneself. And not just to be surrounded by music, but the chance to be immersed in some of the most beautiful music written in any tradition. Choir singing offers people who would not be comfortable alone on stage the opportunity to sing without embarrassment. In addition, the barriers to entry are often very low. In some places one can join a choir with no audition, without previous singing experience, without being able to read music, and with no greater commitment than to show up.

Singing with Others: Because It Brings Us Together

Ensemble singing brings people together in a very literal sense: they all get into the same room to sing together. In this it is like other forms of shared music making that rely on close physical contact. Is singing together any different in this respect from playing in an instrumental group? One obvious difference between singers and other musicians is that ensemble singers pronounce words in unison. Singing the same words at the same time as others might enhance the communal aspect of this kind of music-making and make it especially powerful, especially when the song that is sung celebrates shared values, as do hymns, national anthems, and other kinds of choral songs. Certainly, there is something especially powerful about *hearing* words pronounced by a group of people in unison. And a solo singer can be most affecting when heard against a backdrop of united voices.

Leah McLaren, a Canadian journalist living in London, joined a neighborhood choir when she saw an ad for singers in a local café. She had this to say about communal singing:

> Singing in a choir is a transcendent experience – and there aren't many of those in life. It instills gratitude and bliss without the contortions of yoga or hangovers of alcohol. Singing doesn't just make us feel better – it makes us better people. By singing in a group, we choose to recede for a moment from selfish concerns and pursue harmony with those around us.[12]

I fear that it is too optimistic to believe that singing makes us "better people." Yet McLaren is not alone in experiencing a sense of oneness with fellow singers. Stacy Horn, a writer who sings with the Choral Society of Grace Church in New York City, felt a physical "rush" when (to her initial disappointment) she was assigned a "Soprano 2" part and experienced singing in harmony for the first time from one of the choir's "middle" voices: "I was completely in the power of the sound we were making together and I just stood there, afraid to move, thinking, *Don't end, don't end, don't end.*" She found the experience profoundly moving: "Two notes and I went from a state of complete misery and lonesomeness to such an astonishing sense of communion it was like I'd never sung with the choir before."[13]

Thinkers in different traditions have tried to make sense of the way that communal singing serves to connect the subjective (the individual singer) with the social (the voices and bodies of the group). Zuckerkandl has argued that different interrelations between people are created by singing as opposed to speaking. The spoken word presumes an "other" – the person spoken to, set against the person speaking, and these two face each other as separate individuals. Yet when tones are added to words and individual speech becomes communal singing, individuals who had previously faced one another are transformed into one group. When we sing as part of a group, we perceive the feeling of our own vocal activity within our bodies, and we hear the tones we make combining with those made by others around us. As Zuckerkandl describes it, "the dividing line between myself and others loses its sharpness."[14]

"House of the Rising Sun" (Redux)

Alan Lomax captured a moment in the history of the song "House of the Rising Sun" when he recorded 16-year-old Georgia Turner singing it in Kentucky in 1937. She couldn't remember where she learned the song and no one is sure why she chose it to sing for Lomax. The people who knew her remember that she sang it and other songs frequently throughout her day, while doing her chores and going about her business.

As far as I know, there is no record of anyone asking Georgia why she sang or whom she was singing for. Certainly, she is not known to have aspired to sing professionally. Maybe no one asked because the inner life of a poor teenage girl was not seen to hold much interest. Or maybe no one asked because it seemed obvious: people sing to give a concrete form to inarticulate feelings, hopes, fears, and desires. We borrow the eloquence and musicality of lyricists and composers to express, in a way we could not manage unaided, how we really feel.

Perhaps I have been asking the wrong question. I have framed this chapter around the question "Why sing?" And "Why sing?" implies "Why not sing?" In other words, the way I have set up the question suggests that singing is a choice. It is something we could opt to do or not to do, like playing tennis or eating cupcakes. But what if singing is not an option we choose for varying reasons, but a necessity that is channeled in various ways? If so, then the question should be "Sing when?" or "Why be silent?" rather than "Why sing?" If singing is a necessity or a compulsion, it might help account for the persistence of vocal practices that resemble singing (but are not defined as singing) in cultures where secular music is discouraged. More trivially, it might help explain why people have been known to sing (sometimes tunelessly) when no one else is around to hear them.

Notes

1 Elena Passarello, *Let Me Clear My Throat* (Louisville, KY: Sarabande Books, 2012), 154.
2 "Why Singing in a Choir Might Be Good for You," December 5, 2013, www.brookes.ac.uk/about-brookes/news/choir-research/ (accessed December 12, 2014).
3 Betty A. Bailey and Jane W. Davidson, "Effects of Group Singing and Performance for Marginalized and Middle-class Singers," *Psychology of Music* 33:3 (2005), 269–303.
4 W.T. Fitch, "The Biology and Evolution of Music: A Comparative Perspective," *Cognition* 100:1 (2006), 173–215.
5 Charles Hartshorne, *Born to Sing: An Interpretation and World Survey of Bird Song* (Bloomington: Indiana University Press, 1973); and David Rothenberg, *Why Birds Sing: A Journey into the Mystery of Birdsong* (New York: Basic Books, 2006).
6 Hartshorne, *Born to Sing.*
7 Quoted in Raymond Arsenault, *The Sound of Freedom: Marian Anderson, the Lincoln Memorial, and the Concert that Awakened America* (New York: Bloomsbury Press, 2010), 46.
8 Gracyk, *I Wanna Be Me,* 181.
9 Cone, *The Composer's Voice,* 79.
10 Mladen Dolar, *A Voice and Nothing More* (Cambridge, MA: MIT Press, 2006), 22.
11 See Allan Bloom, trans., *The Republic of Plato,* 2nd ed. (New York: Basic Books, 1991), 344–48.
12 Leah McLaren, "Why I Joined a Choir (and Why It's the Best)," *The Globe and Mail,* March 14, 2014, www.theglobeandmail.com/arts/music/why-i-joined-a-choir-and-why-its-the-best/article17494326/ (accessed December 10, 2014).
13 Stacy Horn, *Imperfect Harmony: Finding Happiness Singing with Others* (Chapel Hill: Algonquin Books, 2013), 31–32.
14 Zuckerkandl, *Man the Musician,* 28.

Index